WARRIOR NOTES HOMESCHOOLING

Phonics 2
2nd Grade
Units 4-6

Warrior Notes Homeschooling

Second Grade Curriculum: Phonics, Language Arts, and Writing

A concise and balanced curriculum that will help build a solid foundation in phonics with God's love at the forefront.

1 John 4:19 TPT
Our love for others is our grateful response to the love God first demonstrated to us.

1 Corinthians 13:2 TPT
And if I were to have the gift of prophecy with a profound understanding of God's hidden secrets, and if I possessed unending supernatural knowledge, and if I had the greatest gift of faith that could move mountains, but have never learned to love, then I am nothing.

Table of Contents

Introduction

Phonics, language arts, and writing

Phonics instruction is most commonly referred to as a strategy that links letter sounds and their spelling. Early use of phonics emphasizes pictures and sounds and other strategies like sounding out letters and letter combinations to form sounds. The basic phonetic process is that each letter represents a sound, and the letter sounds compose words. The English language has 44 phonetic sounds. So how do we teach phonics? We teach children that an alphabetic letter represents a sound. When we put sounds of letters together, we form words. Mastering phonics at an early age is beneficial for a child's reading ability.

Overview

Second Grade Phonics is a 36-week lesson plan that equals 180 days of instruction. The focus is on phonics, grammar, reading comprehension, spelling, and writing. Each day the curriculum will focus on increasing the knowledge of letter sounds and blends as children move from simple to more complex words. Practice is divided between reading and writing.

Using this course

Daily lessons consist of instruction and practice. The top portion of the page provides examples for you to use as teaching examples. The bottom portion provides practice for your child to apply the skills being taught. Certain lessons include dictation. There is a detailed example of a dictation lesson in the back of this book. The suggested time for completing the lesson is approximately 20 - 25 minutes.

Course Objectives

Second grade phonics objectives consist of students learning how to apply consonant blends and digraph vowel pair sounds to more complex reading passages and writing. Second grade students will work with both reading and writing.

Notes for the parent/teacher

At the beginning of each unit there will be detailed instructions and tips to help you deliver the lessons for that unit.

Scope and Sequence

Unit 4
Weeks 19-24 we will focus on adding prefixes and suffixes to words, homonyms, and
syllables

Week 19: Adding prefixes and suffixes to base words

Week 20: Suffix spelling rules

Week 21: Homonyms

Week 22: Syllable Introduction

Week 23: Syllable rules

Week 24: Review

Unit 5
Weeks 25-30 we will focus on grammar and parts of speech

Week 25: Using proper punctuation

Week 26: Abbreviations

Week 27: Nouns, verbs, adjectives, and adverbs

Week 28: Simple subject and predicate

Week 29: Sentence diagram practice

Week 30: Review

Unit 6
Weeks 31-36 will focus on writing

Week 31: Understanding different types of writing

Week 32: Writing genres: Poetry, fiction, nonfiction, and drama

Week 33: Process of Writing a composition

Week 34: Writing an opinion/persuasive composition

Week 35: Writing an informative/explanatory composition

Week 36: Writing poems

Answer Keys

Resources

Unit 4
Week 19-24

Adding prefixes and suffixes to words, homonyms, and syllables

Unit 4 Instructions

This unit focuses on word parts (prefixes, suffixes, and syllables) and homonyms. Your child will be working closely with a variety of word parts, learning to segment and create new words.

An affix is a prefix and suffix. Affixes are word parts that are added to a base word. A base word is a word that stands alone. Words like love, peace, and joy are base words. When you add an affix to a word it changes the meaning. If I add the prefix (un) and the suffix (ly) to love, I get the word unlovely. It is important that your child begin to memorize the meanings of the basic affixes as they will come across these often in their reading. Knowing the definitions helps your child figure out the meanings of larger words. One suggestion is to make flash cards. Another way to practice is to look for words with affixes in the newspaper, a magazine, books, or even signs. Practice figuring out the meanings based on their prefixes or suffixes. This is a great way to practice and learn the meanings of the various affixes.

Homonyms are composed of both homophones and homographs. Homophones are words that sound the same but have different meanings and different spellings. Homographs are words that are spelled the same but have different meanings and sometimes different pronunciations. There are many ways to provide extra practice for your child. Using index cards, write the homonym on one card and the definition or a picture on the other. These cards can be used to play Memory, Go Fish, or even Pictionary. Understanding homonyms will aid in your child's comprehension.

Syllabication is the division of words into word parts. This is a skill that must be learned for a reader to be successful. Successful readers don't just memorize words. While it is important that basic sight words be memorized and then built upon, a reader will encounter larger words as reading progresses. Syllabication helps your child break words into chunks and successfully read those larger words. Every syllable will have one vowel sound. There are many ways to practice syllabication. One way is to count jaw drops. Each time a syllable is spoken your jaw will drop. Have your child place a hand under the jaw and say the word melon. Then count how many times the jaw drops. Another way is to clap each time a word part is heard. Practice can be continued with sticks, spoons, stomps, and hums.

It is recommended that your child read a book of choice for thirty minutes a day. The more reading practice, the better the reader. Reading together is a great way to allow your child to practice while still being able to provide support!

Prefix, Suffix, and Base Words

Base Words

A base word is a word in its smallest part. It stands alone.
A prefix or suffix can be added to a base word and will usually change the meaning of the word.

care ♡ 　　　　　 ▱ test

Prefix

A prefix is a word part added to the **beginning** of a word.

pre + test = pretest

Pre means before. When we add it to test we change the meaning. Now we have a test that is taken before the main test.

Suffix

A suffix is a word part added to the **end** of a word.

care + **less** = careless

Less means without. When we add it to care we change the meaning. Now we have someone without care.

Highlight the base word and draw a line under
the prefix or suffix in each word below

incomplete	healthy	prevent
restore	subway	inexpensive
reuse	prayed	talking
stronger	cleanest	safely
restful	effortless	unpack

Affixes and Base Words

Choose a prefix and base word from the boxes below to make a new word. Write the new word and draw a picture.

Prefixes	Word: _____	Base Words
un		heat
pre		cook
re		fair

Word: _____

Word: _____

Choose a base word and a suffix from the boxes below to make a new word. Write the new word and draw a picture.

Base Words	Word: _____	Suffixes
thank		less
mix		ful
cheer		er

Word: _____

Word: _____

The Lord is for _____ .

Prefixes

un - not	**re** - again	**in** - not, opposite
un + tie = **un**tie	**re** + build = **re**build	**in** + correct = **in**correct
meaning: not tied	meaning: build again	meaning: not correct

pre - before	**sub** - below
pre + order = **pre**order	**sub** + way = **sub**way
meaning: order before	meaning: travel under

Draw a line to match the prefix to the base word.
Write the new word.

un   read   _____ reread _____

re   pay   _____

in   true   _____

pre   title   _____

re   valid   _____

sub   act   _____

More Prefixes

Choose which prefix will correctly complete the word.

de   dis   im

Prefix	Base word	New Word
dis	respect	disrespect
	crease	
	mature	
	flate	
	patient	
	code	
	agree	
	connect	

God defeats _____'s enemies.

Prefixes

mid - middle	mis - wrong, bad	non - without
mid + day = midday	mis + deed = misdeed	non + stop = nonstop
meaning: middle of the day	meaning: bad deed	meaning: without stopping

Add a prefix to the word to finish the sentence.

mid   mis   non

Everyone should be asleep by _____.
(night)

The yogurt we buy is _____.
(fat)

We have to be careful that we do not _____ people.
(judge)

I like to read _____ books that have facts.
(fiction)

He couldn't find the letter because it was _____.
(filed)

We lost our canoe paddle _____.
(stream)

The baby's words sounded like _____.
(sense)

Vowel Suffixes

er - compare	ed - past tense	ing - action
sweet + **er** = sweet**er**	jump + **ed** = jump**ed**	add + **ing** = add**ing**

able - capable	est - compare	ible - able
like + **able** = like**able**	warm + **est** = warm**est**	flex + **ible** = flex**ible**

y - state of, condition	es - more than one
fluff + **y** = fluff**y**	globe + **es** = glob**es**

Base Word	er	est
tall		
long		
short		
small		

Underline the suffix. Write the definition of the word.

swinging _____

responsible _____

foxes _____

painted _____

washable _____

windy _____

_____ is an overcomer in Jesus.

Consonant Suffixes

ly - state of, condition slow + **ly** = slowly	**ful** - full of slow + **ful** = truthful
less - without sun + **less** = sunless	**ness**- state of, condition kind + **ness** = kindness
ment - action ship + **ment** = shipment	**ion** - action invent + **ion** = invention

Color the suffixes that correctly completes the word.

glad [ly] [ion]   cup [ment] [ful]

end [less] [ful]   sad [ness] [ion]

glad [ment] [ness]   count [ly] [less]

agree [ly] [ment]   bright [less] [ly]

select [ion] [less]   develop [ly] [ment]

rest [ness] [ful]   subtract [ness] [ion]

Vowel and Consonant Suffixes

or - person	ous - quality of	wise - relating to
direct + **or** = director	zeal + **ous** = zealous	other + **wise** = otherwise
meaning: a person who directs	meaning: quality of having zeal	meaning: relating to another way

Add one of these suffixes to the bold words in each sentence.

or ous wise

Folding the paper in **length.** What fold? _____

A closet that **elevat**es. What is it? _____

A person who **act**s. What are they? _____

We hiked in a lot of **mountain**s.

What was it? _____

I found myself in an area where there was **danger.**

What was it? _____

I go around from right to left like a **clock.**

How do I go? _____

It takes **courage** to do something when frightened.

What is it? _____

The Lord bring joy to _____.

Prefix and Suffix Review

Highlight the base word and underline the
prefix or suffix in each word.

inspector   unsafe

retry   suitable   subside

permissible   impolite

latches   misspell   weakness

crosswise   danced

colder   invisible   richest

                throwing   messy

preview   midweek   powerful

quickly   defog

placement   homeless   adventurous

nondairy   dislike

decoration

Crossword Review

Highlight the base words and underline the prefix or suffix in the word bank. Then find and circle the words in the crossword.

N	T	Q	I	P	T	K	L	I	K	E	W	I	S	E	I	E	U	N	B
Y	J	W	N	A	F	U	C	V	V	Z	C	Q	C	G	K	A	B	G	Y
I	Q	D	G	Y	R	U	J	Q	Y	R	G	R	A	C	E	F	U	L	W
Z	Z	H	X	J	L	C	D	I	X	P	Z	T	Y	O	Y	O	M	V	I
N	U	T	C	Y	X	L	Z	O	O	V	R	I	H	O	Z	X	P	L	S
P	S	L	D	U	G	N	W	Y	P	F	O	N	A	A	Q	K	Y	X	U
T	L	D	I	D	I	S	T	R	U	S	T	L	J	N	J	J	Y	E	B
D	D	I	X	B	W	D	Z	P	G	E	H	E	V	L	F	I	Z	A	F
J	A	R	K	T	E	S	O	F	T	N	E	S	S	W	M	O	V	Z	K
O	R	Y	I	E	N	W	N	Q	D	B	R	E	U	T	K	L	Q	I	O
H	K	W	E	U	D	B	I	O	R	A	S	H	E	S	E	L	E	S	S
W	E	Q	Z	J	F	Y	A	S	M	A	O	L	C	H	I	N	T	X	L
X	R	G	N	O	N	F	A	T	G	S	S	B	V	T	C	V	O	Z	F
L	Z	C	Q	Y	U	S	E	L	E	S	S	H	F	H	O	I	E	Y	I
E	U	J	F	Y	Z	T	F	H	N	M	M	O	S	C	L	S	O	D	L
F	N	T	J	M	N	S	N	U	N	W	I	S	E	S	D	I	U	B	L
W	R	E	P	L	A	Y	F	O	D	C	I	W	S	O	L	T	Y	P	I
Z	A	L	I	K	E	D	K	L	R	S	K	S	H	M	Y	O	O	J	N
Q	V	M	Y	Y	Y	Q	G	F	U	X	Q	I	E	U	C	R	S	D	G
F	G	Y	X	B	W	R	H	I	Y	D	R	C	P	D	G	I	S	H	I

Word Bank

likewise	distrust	darker	nonfat	coldly
bumpy	replay	useless	unwise	liked
graceful	filling	rashes	visitor	softness

Week 20

Prefixes and Suffixes

A **prefix** is added to the **beginning** of a word.
A **suffix** is a added to the **end** of a word.

Prefix - Base Word - Suffix

un - help - ful

Vowel Suffixes

-es (more than one)   watch + **es** = watches

-able (can do)   love + **able** = lovable

-ible (can do)   invinc + **ible** = invincible

Use -**able** when the word is complete. Use -**ible** for a word part.

Underline the suffix. Write the definition of the word.
The first one is done for you.

boxes _____ more than one box _____

washable _____

churches _____

incredible _____

profitable _____

glasses _____

sensible _____

breakable _____

dishes _____

potatoes _____

responsible _____

Suffixes

Write the correct suffix to complete the word in each sentence.

tion   ment   ness

We have to come into _____ with God's plan for us.
(agree)

In the Bible, kids made fun of Elisha's _____.
(bald)

Jesus healed a man's _____ by putting mud on his eyes.
(blind)

Our lives should be a _____ of Jesus.
(reflect)

Our _____ includes a president and a vice-president.
(govern)

We are made in the _____ of God.
(like)

Doug's _____ equation was correct.
(subtract)

The _____ for a couch is about eight feet.
(measure)

_____ leans on God's understanding.

Suffix Rule: Double the Consonant

Double the consonant when:
- a base word has a **short vowel** and **ends with a consonant**.
  (Do not double w, x, or y.)

  pop ⟶ popping

- a base word has more than one syllable, the **second syllable** has a **short vowel** and **ends with a consonant**.

  tip ⟶ tipping

Complete each word by adding the suffix -ed and -ing.

base word	ed suffix	ing suffix
plan	planned	planning
clap		
trim		
spot		
cram		
chop		

Suffix Rule: Keep the y

Keep the **(y)** when:
- a base word ends in a vowel + **(y)**.

play ⟶ playing

- a suffix starting with **(i)** is being added to the base word.

carry ⟶ carrying

Color the words that are written correctly green.
Color the words that are written incorrectly red.

say	pray	try
saing	praying	triing

marry	stay	enjoy
marrying	staing	enjoying

buy	fly	apply
buying	flying	appliing

Suffix Rule: Change the y to an i

Change the **(y)** to an **(i)** when a base word ends in a consonant + **(y)**.

duty ⟶ dutiful

Rule Exception: Keep the **(y)** when the suffix starts with an **(i)**.

dry ⟶ drying

Circle the word that has the correct spelling for each sentence.

The Lord's gifts are very _____.
(plentyful / plentiful)

The angel _____ of the Lord always do God's will.
(armyes / armies)

The _____ children are always singing.
(joyful / joiful)

The baby didn't stop _____ for two hours.
(crying/criing)

Carol _____ to make the kite fly.
(tryed / tried)

The family decided it was _____ to leave than to stay.
(riskyer / riskier)

The _____ dolphin made us laugh.
(beautyful / beautiful)

Suffix Rule: Change ie to y

When a word ends in **(ie)**, change **(ie)** to a **(y)**
if the suffix starts with **(i)**.

tie ———→ tying

Add -ing to the word **lie** and write a sentence.

_____

_____

_____

Add -ing to the word **tie** and write a sentence.

_____

_____

_____

Add -ing to the word **die** and write a sentence.

_____

_____

_____

_____ delights in the Lord.

Suffix Rule: Drop the Silent e

When a base word ends in a silent (e), drop the (e) and add a **vowel suffix**.

smile ⟶ smil**ing**

Choose the right word from the box that completes the sentence and write it on the line with the -ing suffix.

bake	make	drive	take	write	hide	ride

My dad was _____ the car over a bridge.

The baby is _____ his nap.

We are _____ cards for the nursing home.

Sofia's little brother was _____ under the bed.

We are going to go _____ at the ranch.

You can smell the _____ bread all over the house.

She is _____ her name ten times.

Suffix Rule: Keep the Silent e

Keep the silent (e) when:
- a base word ends in a silent (e) and it is a **consonant suffix**.

active ⟶ actively

- a base word ends in (ee) or (ye).

eye ⟶ eyeing   free ⟶ freeing

- a base word ends in (ce) or (ge) and the suffix starts with an (a) or (o).

notice ⟶ noticeable   outrage ⟶ outrageous

Read the letter and write the underlined words
with the suffix correctly at the bottom.

Dear Fred,

I learned that <u>balance + ing</u> a book on my head is a hard thing

to do. I didn't expect to go to a class. I was <u>piece + ing</u> together

a puzzle. I was <u>eye + ing</u> my next piece when my friend

asked me to go. I said ok. I watched the leader <u>close +ly</u>.

She <u>free + ly</u> gave the lesson. I worked on my balance. I was

glad when I found out they weren't <u>charge + ing</u> for the class.

Sincerely,
Tomas

_____   _____

_____   _____

_____   _____

_____ waits patiently on the Lord.

Suffix Review

Highlight the base word and underline the suffix.

families 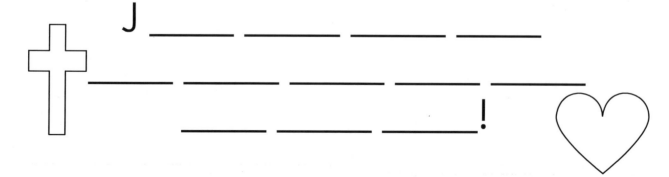	slimming	busier	goodness
likeable	hottest	lovely	reflection
awareness	closely	inspiration	bunnies
responsible	shipment	easier	libraries

Write the bold letters at the bottom to figure out the message.

J ____ ____ ____ ____

____ ____ ____ ____ ____

____ ____ ____ !

Suffix Review

Draw a line to match each base word with a suffix.
Choose five words to write with their definitions.

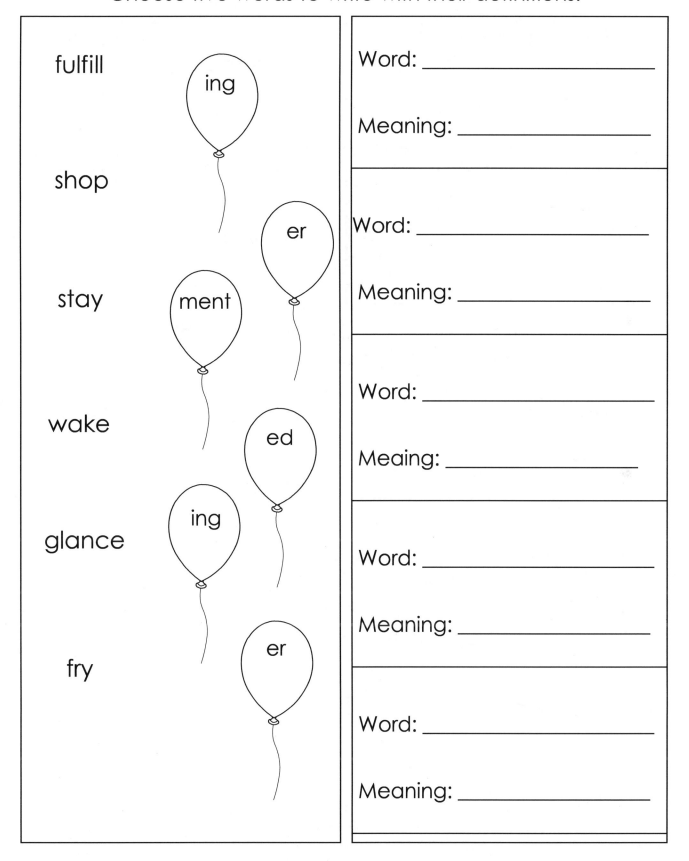

_____ loves others.

Homonyms

Homonyms are words that have the same sound and/or spelling but have a different meaning.

Homophones	Homographs
Words that sound the same BUT have a different spelling.	Words that can sound different BUT have the same spelling.

night   knight

bass   bass

Circle the word pairs that are homophones.
Underline the word pairs that are homographs.

there/their   can/can   wind/wind

park/park   cent/sent

by/buy

who's/whose   night/knight

there/they're   scent/sent

palm/palm   fly/fly

bye/buy

duck/duck

your/you're

Homophones

Words that sound the same BUT have a different spelling.

there  The ant is **there**.	**their** (belongs to)  That is **their** lamb.	**they're** (they are)  **They're** getting married.

Circle the correct homophone for each sentence.

They went to find _____ pet lamb. (there / their / they're)

(There / Their / They're) _____ are five people on the bus.

That is _____ car. (there / their / they're)

(There / Their / They're)_____ going to the beach today.

Those puppies are _____ favorites. (there / their / they're)

Put the books over _____. (there / their / they're)

We told them that _____ a beautiful couple.

(there / their / they're)

_____ has peace from Holy Spirit.

Homophones

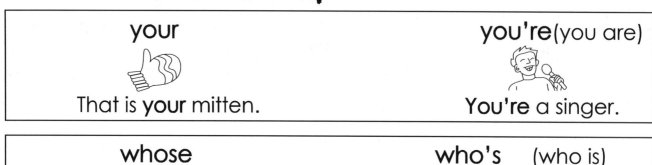

your	you're (you are)
That is **your** mitten.	You're a singer.

whose	who's (who is)
Whose toy truck is this?	Who's that man?

If the sentence is correct, make a check mark on the line. If it is incorrect, write the correct homophone on the line.

your   you're   whose   who's

We want to know **whose** in the picture.   _____

You're going to pass that test.   _____

Who's going to drive with me?   _____

I want to buy **you're** used books.   _____

You're my best friend.   _____

Whose coat is on the couch?   _____

The desk has **your** name on it.   _____

My mom wants to know **whose** eating.   _____

More Homophones

Circle and write the correct homophone for each sentence.

The _____ of applie pie filled the kitchen.

    (cent / scent / sent)

My dad had to _____ school supplies.

    (by / buy / bye)

I was _____ to the kitchen to get a water.

    (cent / scent / sent)

I wanted to sit _____ my friend Charlie in church.

    (by / buy / bye)

It takes more than one _____ to buy carrots.

    (cent / scent / sent)

I waved _____ to my cousins when they left.

    (by / buy / bye)

We have to drive _____ the bank on our way home.

    (by / buy / bye)

Holy Spirit gives joy to _____ .

Homographs

Some **homographs** have the same spelling and sounds,
BUT they have different meanings.

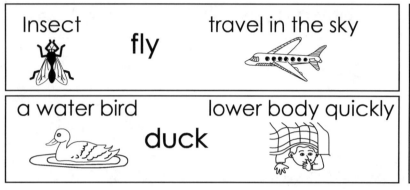

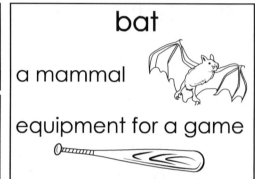

Choose the right homograph from above
to complete the sentences below.

There was a _____ sitting on the airplane when we had to _____ to Colorado.

I told my friend Kevin to _____ when the _____ flew near him.

We saw a _____ flying around the light as Tommy went to _____ for his team.

Write two sentence using the different forms of the word: **bat.**

_____

_____

_____

_____

More Homographs

can	park	palm
ability	put in a space	tree
container	place to visit	part of hand

Choose the right homograph from above
to complete the sentences below.

I hit the _____ of
my hand on the _____
tree and it was sharp.

I _____ play my
guitar while I drink a _____
of orange juice.

We had to _____ the car before we could go hiking in
the state _____.

Write two sentence using the different forms of the word: **can.**

_____

_____

_____

_____

Holy Spirit gives patience to _____.

Homographs

Some homographs have the same spelling, BUT
they have different sounds and meanings.

mouth open		love
	agape	
unit of time		tiny
	minute	

moped
motor bike
unhappy

Choose the homograph from the word box to correctly
complete the sentence. Read the sentence aloud.

agape	minute	moped

The puppy was so _____ it was hard to see.

It was _____ love that brought Jesus to earth for us.

She rode on the _____ with her friend Donna.

The squirrel _____ around because he lost his peanut.

George's mouth was _____ when he saw his surprise.

We had one _____ to win the game.

More Homographs

wind	tear	buffet
Air blowing	to cry	to hit over and over

Make a clock work	rip a paper	a meal

Choose the homograph from the word box to correctly complete the sentence. Read the sentence aloud.

wind	tear	buffet

I went to a _____ to eat with my family.

The _____ is blowing the trees back and forth.

They saw the waves _____ the wall over and over.

The movie made me _____ up because it was sad.

My dad has to _____ up our clock every night.

There was a _____ in my paper so I threw it away.

Holy Spirit gives kindness to _____.

Homonym Review

Read the story two times
Cross out the incorrect homonyms.

They decided to go to the beach. They were excited. They could smell the **cent** of suntan lotion. The **wind** began to blow as they carried **there** chairs to the beach. The sky was getting darker by the **minute**. They saw a **minute** ant headed for an ant hill. **There** was a **moped** parked on the sidewalk. Someone had dropped a **bat** on the ground. They wondered **who's** it was. As they walked, they went **buy** the lifeguard. He told them that a storm was coming. He looked at them and said, "Watch **your** umbrella. It might blow away." That's when they saw the life guards leave **they're** posts as the rain started. They decided to go home. One boy had a **tear** in his eye. His mom said, "Don't worry, **your** going to get **your** chance to swim tomorrow.

Fix the homonyms the are not used correctly. Write them below.

_____   _____

_____   _____

_____   _____

Homonym Puzzle Review

Draw a line to match the sentence to the correct homonym.

_____ going to get a family picture

I saw my dog wave _____.

I needed one _____ to buy an apple.

agape

they're

duck

cent

bye

who's

I told my friend to _____ so he didn't get hit.

_____ going to watch the game?

God's love for us is _____ love.

Write two sentences using the different forms of the word: **tear.**

_____

_____

_____

_____

_____

_____

Week 22

God has plans for _____.

Syllables

A syllable is a word part. Every syllable must have one vowel. It can have two vowels if they are a pair, and one is silent.

tub   fan   paint

Read each one syllable word and highlight the vowel sounds. Practice your cursive by tracing and writing the word two times

map   *map*

_____   _____

truck   truck

_____   _____

snap   *snap*

_____   _____

hum   hum

_____   _____

Why do each of these words have only one syllable?

_____

_____

_____

Counting Syllables

You can count syllables by the vowel sounds you hear.

snout

Snout has one vowel sound.
Snout has one syllable.

sneaker

Sneaker has two vowel sounds.
Sneaker has two syllables.

You divide syllables by drawing a line between the syllables

sneak/er   dream/ing   sweet/ie   tar/get

Read each word and highlight the vowel sounds.

Circle the number of syllables in each word.

basket	1	2	mug	1	2
flower	1	2	cookie	1	2
test	1	2	kazoo	1	2
lemon	1	2	cube	1	2
bench	1	2	airplane	1	2

Practice writing sentences with 2-syllable words.
Trace and write the cursive sentence on the line.

She wore a <u>necklace</u>.

She wore a necklace.

He rode a <u>stallion</u>.

He rode a stallion.

God prospers _____.

Open Syllables

An open syllable has one vowel and does not have a consonant at the end. The vowel sound is long.

<u>me</u>	<u>we</u>	tem/<u>po</u>	<u>pa</u>/per

Read each word and highlight the **open** syllable in each word.

e / ven	pi / lot	li / on	de / frost
hel / lo	stu / dent	mu / sic	a / pron
bo / nus	be / yond	car / go	be / gin
lo / cate	mo / ment	ho / tel	u / nit

Read and highlight the open syllable.
Write each word in print and cursive.

re / cite	recite	*recite*
	_____	_____
po / lo	polo	*polo*
	_____	_____
pro / tect	protect	*protect*
	_____	_____

Closed Syllables

A closed syllable has a short vowel sound
and ends with a consonant.

<u>pig</u>

<u>dog</u>

<u>mon</u>/key

Read each word and highlight the **closed** syllable in each word.

den / im	hu / man	pro / tect	col / ic
ro / dent	hab / it	hap / pen	ba / sis
fro / zen	sol / id	ped / al	lem /on
si / ren	ham / mer	rob / in	cat / nap

Read and highlight the closed syllable.
Write each word in print and cursive.

in / flate   inflate   *inflate*

_____   _____

hel / met   helmet   *helmet*

_____   _____

wed / ding   wedding   *wedding*

_____   _____

God has a future for _____.

Vowel + Consonante + Syllables

A vowel + consonant + e syllable has a long vowel and a silent e.

b<u>ale</u>   c<u>ape</u>   pan/c<u>ake</u>

Unscramble the following words. Write the divided syllables. Highlight the vowel + consonant + e in each word.

What a volcano does: dlxeepo _____ / _____

How things are the same: reapomc _____ / _____

Something sweet to eat: ckeaupc_____ / _____

When the sun comes up: erinssu _____ / _____

When you ask for help: cevida _____ / _____

When you are out of the sun: desnii _____ / _____

When you don't understand: secfuno _____ / _____

Word Bank

sun / rise   in / side   ex / plode   con / fuse

ad / vice   cup / cake   com / pare

Vowel Team Syllables

A vowel team syllable has two vowels next to each other.
The vowel team makes only one vowel sound.

train   tie   a/sleep

Read each word and highlight the vowel sounds.
Circle the number of syllables in each word.

see	1	2	flounder	1	2
enjoy	1	2	window	1	2
await	1	2	day	1	2
outbreak	1	2	needle	1	2
weapon	1	2	flea	1	2

Practice writing sentences with 2-syllable words.
Write the sentence on the line.

The <u>crayon</u> is purple.

_____

God is <u>faithful</u>.

_____

The <u>peacock</u> is colorful.

_____

God protects _____ from harm.

R-Controlled Syllables

An r-controlled syllable has a vowel that is followed by an (r).
The (r) changes the sound of the vowel.

fe/ver	or/bit	re/turn

Read the sentences to find the words with the
r-controlled syllables and write the word on the line.
Highlight the r-controlled syllable sound.

We used ginger in our recipe. _____ginger_____

I went to the barber for a haircut. _____

That artwork is beautiful. _____

Ellie was certain that she was saved. _____

Jesus brings us comfort. _____

I can bring my Bible to church. _____

A tiger has black stripes. _____

I like peach flavor in my tea. _____

The chipmunk ate five acorns. _____

Consonant + le Syllables

A consonant + le syllable has a consonant followed by (le).
The consonant + (le) comes at the end of the word.

twin/<u>kle</u>   cat/<u>tle</u>   mar/<u>ble</u>

Solve the clues by using the words in the word bank.
Write the word and highlight the consonant + le.

Word Bank
grumble
waddle
freckles
struggle
nibble
jungle
people

A place where tigers and
monkeys live

_____

Little brown dots on
your skin

_____

Who we are called to
love

_____

Eating small bites

_____

When something is causing a
problem we sometimes:

_____

The way a duck
walks

_____

When we complain we:

_____

Choose one word from the word bank and write it in a sentence.

_____

_____

God has given _____ hope.

Multi-Syllabic Words

Many English words have more than one syllable.
We call these multi-syllabic words.
You can count them by listening for the vowel sound.

chick (1)   pret/zel (2)   spa/ghet/ti (3)

Highlight the vowel sounds and circle the
number of syllables in each word.

notebook	1	2	3	donut	1	2	3
skew	1	2	3	elephant	1	2	3
octopus	1	2	3	mask	1	2	3
butterfly	1	2	3	taco	1	2	3
evergreen	1	2	3	almost	1	2	3
queen	1	2	3	detective	1	2	3
thanksgiving	1	2	3	once	1	2	3
softly	1	2	3	bunny	1	2	3
jellyfish	1	2	3	strawberry	1	2	3
clam	1	2	3	broccoli	1	2	3

Challenge:

How many syllables are there in the word: dandelion? _____

Multi-Syllabic Words

Trace the divided syllables and write if it is open or closed.

Word	syllable 1	open/closed	syllable 2	open/closed
humid	*hu*	open	*mid*	closed
hallway			*way*	
study				
basic				
castle	*cas*		*tle*	
preschool				

Word	syllable 1	open/closed	syllable 2	open/closed	syllable 3	open/closed
vacation	*va*				*tion*	
location			*ca*		*tion*	
computer	*com*		*pu*		*ter*	
ladybug	*la*					
regular						
potato	*po*		*ta*		*to*	

Week 23

Syllables Rule #1

When dividing syllables, r-controlled vowels (**ar, er, ir, or,** and **ur**) are partners. They always stay together. You divide the syllable after the pair.

harvest = har / vest

Circle the r-controlled vowel pair. Then write the two syllables.

garden	_____ / _____
forget	_____ / _____
argue	_____ / _____
target	_____ / _____
worship	_____ / _____
party	_____ / _____
plural	_____ / _____
burger	_____ / _____
urchin	_____ / _____
bargain	_____ / _____

Syllable Rule #2

When dividing syllables, all syllables have only **one** vowel sound.

pen/cil   pic/nic   cac/tus

Draw a line to divide the syllables and highlight the vowel sound in each. There should only be **one** vowel sound in each syllable.

can/did   velvet   odor

laughter   excite   finish

exam   sandwich   doctor

basket   below   gavel

tiger   until   zebra

robin   magnet   cabin

Choose one word from the list and write a sentence.

_____

_____

_____

_____

Jesus goes before _____.

Syllable Rule #3

When dividing syllables, divide a two syllable
word between twin letters.

cherries = cher/ries   kettle = ket/tle

Highlight the words that have two syllables and
divided between the twin letters.

car/rot   ill   puppy

scissors   funny   egg

comma   floss   messy

jiggle   hammer   cuff

dress   sparrow   million

lettuce   fizz   little

dinner   shell   puzzle

Choose one word from the list and write a sentence.

_____

_____

_____

_____

Syllable Rule #4

When dividing syllables, divide the word between two middle consonants when there is a vowel on each side.

d e <u>nt</u> i s t = den / tist   ma<u>rk</u>er = mar/ker

Fill in the sentences with these two-syllable words and write the word with the syllables divided.

insect   subject   absent   falcon

wisdom   plastic   chapter   napkin

The _____ / _____flew through the air with its dinner.

The fear of the Lord is the beginning of _____ / _____.

Matt laid the _____ / _____on his lap at dinner.

A bee is an _____ /_____that makes honey.

My favorite _____ / _____to study is Bible.

I read a whole _____ / _____in my book.

I was _____ /_____from choir practice last Saturday.

The _____ /_____fork broke and I had to get another one.

Syllable Rule #5

When dividing syllables, divide <u>after the consonant</u> when the vowel is **short**.

 w a g / o n

When dividing syllables, divide <u>before the consonant</u> when the vowel is **long**.

 u / n i t

Color the rectangle that shows the correct division of syllables.

open	o/pen	op/en

vacant	va/cant	vac/ant

talent	ta/lent	tal/ent

tiger	ti/ger	tig/er

given	gi/ven	giv/en

finish	fi/nish	fin/ish

baby	ba/by	bab/y

seven	se/ven	sev/en

robin	ro/bin	rob/in

super	su/per	sup/er

comic	co/mic	com/ic

lemon	le/mon	lem/on

pilot	pi/lot	pil/ot

Friday	Fri/day	Frid/ay

visit	vi/sit	vis/it

music	mu/sic	mus/ic

Syllable Rule #6

When dividing syllables, divide between compound words.

s u n / l i g h t   c o b / w e b   c a t / f i s h

Match the words to create a new word. Divide the syllables.

foot   cake   ___foot/ball___

rain   ball   _____ / _____

jelly   bow   _____ / _____

snow   brush   _____ / _____

butter   cake   _____ / _____

pan   fish   _____ / _____

cup   man   _____ / _____

sun   flower   _____ / _____

cow   fly   _____ / _____

tooth   boy   _____ / _____

The Lord is faithful to _____.

Syllable Rule #7

When dividing syllables, digraphs (ck, ch, sh, th, wh) stay together. ro/<u>ck</u>et	When dividing syllables, vowel teams (ai, ea, oa, oe, ee, ue, oo) stay together. bal/l<u>oo</u>n

Write each syllable and write the word. Highlight the digraph.

Word	1st syllable	2nd syllable	word
jacket	jack	et	jacket
ostrich			
thermos			
sunshine			
whisper			

Write each syllable and write the word. Highight the vowel team.

Word	1st syllable	2nd syllable	word
remain			
payee			
pursue			
upload			
eager			

Syllable Rule #8

When dividing syllables, consonant blends
(cl, thr, sp, str, sk, pr, lt, mp, dr, lf, ld) stay together.

sta<u>mp</u>/ing   <u>pre</u>/sent   hun/<u>dre</u>d

Write each syllable and write the word. Highlight the blends.

Word	1st syllable	2nd syllable	word
jolted			
grumpy			
laundry			
skipper			
spinal			
herald			
cluster			
pretzel			
skipper			
threaten			
myself			

The Lord fights for _____.

Syllable Rule #9

When dividing syllables, divide after a prefix (un, im, pre, in, re).

<u>un</u>/fair   <u>in</u>/spect   <u>pre</u>/pare

Draw a line to divide the syllables and highlight the prefix.

un/tidy   reread   invent

prefer   image   unwell

intend   unpaid   rebuy

insist   precise    impose

unwrap   predict   return

redo   impress   unsafe

Choose one word from the list and write a sentence.

_____

_____

_____

Syllable Rule #10

When dividing syllables, divide before the consonant + (le).

ap/ple   ea/gle   tur/tle

Fill in the sentences with these two-syllable words
and divide the words into syllables.

battle   candle   beagle   humble
maple   circle   drizzle   waffle

God lifts up those who _____ /_____ themselves.

I have a lavender oil scented _____ / _____.

The rain began to _____ / _____ from the dark clouds.

My bracelet is a perfect _____ / _____.

I like to eat syrup on my _____ / _____.

We get our syrup from a _____ / _____ tree.

Our pet _____ / _____ likes to howl every night.

We do not _____ / _____ against flesh and blood.

Week 24 _____ loves Jesus.

Prefix Review

Write a prefix for each base word. Then write the whole word.

mid	un	sub	im	pre	dis
de	non	mis	in	re	

A point in the middle   ____point   _____

To say before   ____dict   _____

A boat under the water   ____marine   _____

Not able to stick   ____stick   _____

Not perfect   ____perfect   _____

Not able to activate   ____activate   _____

To paint again   ____paint   _____

To judge in a wrong way   ____judge   _____

Not aware   ____aware   _____

Not active   ____active   _____

No longer appearing   ____appear   _____

Rewrite the words in print and cursive.

midway   *midway*

_____   _____

prevent   *prevent*

_____   _____

Suffix Review

Add the correct suffix to each word. Use the new words to complete the story.

ed	ing	est	er	ible	able
ful	ly	ness	ment	ous	

incred_____   excit_____   courage_____

beauti_____   move_____   enjoy_____

clos_____   cold_____   smel_____

hang_____   sweet_____

Our family went to visit the aquarium. We had been studying

_____ sea creatures and I was _____to

see them in person. The aquarium was _____. The

creatures were full of _____. We had a guide that was

so _____. He took us behind the

scenes so we could get a _____look at the

penguins. It was the _____ room I'd ever been in.

It was very _____. We saw a dolphin

_____around the edge of the pool on our

way to the stingrays. We were _____when

we touched the stingrays. It was a wonderful day!

How was the family brave?

_____

_____

_____

Jesus loves _____.

Suffix Spelling Review

Add the base word to a suffix. Write the word.

Double the Consonant

ham + er = _____   clip + ed = _____

drop + ing = _____   plan + er = _____

Keep the final **e** after **ce** and **ge**

slice +able= _____   courage + ous = _____

peace+ able = _____   outrage + ous = _____

Change **y** to **i** or **ie** to **y**

party + es = _____   body + ly = _____

vie + ing = _____   die + ing = _____

Drop the silent e

time + ing = _____   rule + ing = _____

mute + ing = _____   bite + ing = _____

Keep the y

fly + ing = _____   dry + ing = _____

apply+ ing = _____   supply + ing = _____

Is it Spelled Right?

Color the word that is spelled correctly after adding the suffix.

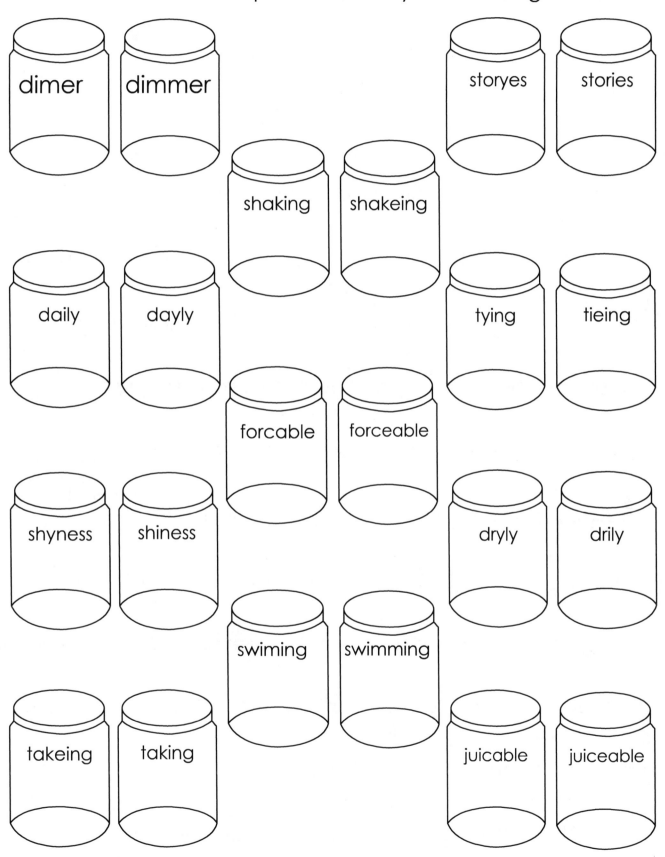

dimer | dimmer

storyes | stories

shaking | shakeing

daily | dayly

tying | tieing

forcable | forceable

shyness | shiness

dryly | drily

swiming | swimming

takeing | taking

juicable | juiceable

Jesus died for _____.

Homophones

Circle the word that will complete the sentence correctly.

I want to (buy / by / bye) a hot pretzel.

(Your / You're) a fabulous artist.

I went to (there / their / they're) youth camp.

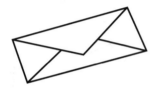
I (scent / sent / cent) a letter to my friend.

(Whose/Who's) your favorite author?

The (scent / sent / cent) of cookies filled the house.

(Whose/Who's) house did we go to last week?

The baby waved (buy / by / bye) to his aunt.

(There / Their / They're) are favorite team.

Casey gave (Your / You're) book to a friend.

I needed one more (scent / sent / cent) to buy the pizza.

The leash is (buy / by / bye) the door.

(There / Their / They're) are no games today.

Homographs

Circle the correct definition of the underlined word.

He wants to <u>fly</u> around the world.

a. an insect   b. travel in the sky

The <u>bat</u> swooped down to catch a bug.

a. an animal   b. equipment to play a game

The <u>wind</u> was so strong it blew my umbrella away.

a. air blowing   b. make a clock work

We took our car to the <u>park</u>.

a. put in a space   b. place to visit

I like to drink my soda from a <u>can</u>.

a. an ability   b. a container

Write the meaning of the underlined word.

Jamie <u>moped</u> all day because he couldn't go to the park.

_____

_____

I burned my <u>palm</u> when I grabbed the hot pan.

_____

_____

God provides for _____.

Syllable Review

Sort the word by the number of syllables.

Word Bank

none	watermelon	pajama	cucumber
lady	helicopter	jigsaw	free
purse	wonderful	sandwich	alligator
wise	television	fantastic	donate

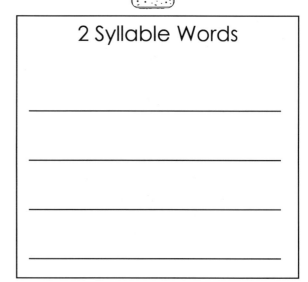

---

1 Syllable Words

_____

_____

_____

_____

2 Syllable Words

_____

_____

_____

_____

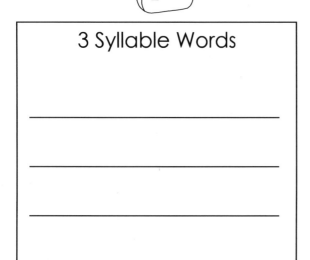

3 Syllable Words

_____

_____

_____

_____

4 Syllable Words

_____

_____

_____

_____

Syllable Review

Divide the syllables in each word.
Color the star that shows if the **first** syllable is open or closed.

umbrella	open closed	fingerprint	open closed
bicycle	open closed	taken	open closed
ponytail	open closed	lemonade	open closed
tomato	open closed	blueberry	open closed
bonus	open closed	grasshopper	open closed
excited	open closed	January	open closed

Divide the syllables in each word. Write the words in cursive twice.

opinion

_____   _____

mimic

_____   _____

forgetful

_____   _____

Syllable Division Review

Divide the syllables and tell which rule supports your answer.

1. R-controlled partners stay together.
2. All syllables have one vowel sound.
3. Divide between twin letters.
4. Divide between two middle consonants.
5. Divide after the consonant when the vowel is short. Divide before the consonant when the vowel is long.
6. Divide between compound words.
7. Digraphs stay together. Vowel teams stay together.
8. Blends stay together.
9. Divide after a prefix.
10. Divide before a consonant + le.

person _____   fabric _____   begin _____

exit _____   shampoo _____   esteem _____

ticklish _____   wildlife _____   itchy _____

uncle _____   subtract _____   market _____

mission _____   fumble _____   comet _____

charcoal _____   frosting _____   number _____

handstand _____   tulip _____   inform _____

mopping _____   teacup _____   pillow _____

Dividing Syllables Review

These syllables are divided incorrectly. Rewrite the word and divide the syllables correctly.

ponytail   pony / tail   _____

written   writt / en   _____

icepack   i / ce / pack   _____

explain   ex / pl / ain   _____

mismatch   mis / ma /tch   _____

flavor   fl / a / vor   _____

whisper   whisp / er   _____

pumpkin   pum / pkin   _____

slipper   sli / pper   _____

frighten   fr / igh / ten   _____

garden   ga / r / den   _____

Choose one word from the list and write a sentence.

_____

_____

_____

Unit 5
Week 25-30

Grammar and parts of speech

Unit 5 Instructions

This unit focuses on grammar and parts of speech. Your child will be working closely with the various parts of a sentence.

A review of punctuation proceeds the learning of apostrophes. Your child will learn how to use apostrophes to show possession, as well as combining two words. When teaching about apostrophes for possession, it is important to review the rule concerning words that already end in (s). If it is a proper noun, just add the apostrophe. If it is a common noun, add an ('s). When combining words, a good way to explain is to share that the apostrophe takes the place of the missing letters. The exceptions to this rule are the words don't and won't. Use magnetic letters, a whiteboard, or paper to practice combining words.

As you work with each part of speech, allow time for practice. Make a parts of speech book with your child. This can be done with a piece of construction paper and plain or lined paper staples inside. When working with nouns and adjectives, take a walk and find as many nouns as you can. Write those down under the noun/adjective pages and illustrate them according to the adjective. An example would be finding a yellow daisy. When working with verbs and adverbs, give commands and have your child do them. An example would be "run quickly". Take a picture and place those pictures on the verb/adverb pages.

Diagramming sentences will help your child create a visual map on how each part of speech works. Having a solid understanding of parts of speech, as well as simple subjects and predicates will aid in diagramming sentences. Consider spending time reviewing the parts of speech, simple subjects, and predicates as you begin diagramming sentences. If you find that your child is struggling, go back and review parts of speech before completing this week. Predictable sentences have been chosen for the second-grade curriculum. This is to help your child master diagramming sentences.

It is recommended that your child read a book of choice for thirty minutes a day. The more reading practice, the better the reader. Reading together is a great way to allow your child to practice while still being able to provide support!

Holy Spirit gives _____ love.

Punctuation Marks

Periods
Periods (.) are used to show a reader when to stop reading.
They go at the end of a sentence.

Question Marks
Question marks (?) are used to show a reader that a question is being asked. They go at the end of a sentence.

?

Exclamation Points
Exclamation points (!) are used to show a reader that there is strong emotion. They go at the end of a sentence.

!

Write in the correct end mark.

Sammy shouted, "Jesus loves me _____"

On Sundays I go to church to worship Jesus _____

Why do tigers have stripes on them _____

Stop the car _____

Jesus is the Son of God _____

Write a sentence using a period.

_____

_____

End Marks

If the punctuation is correct, write a "C" on the line.
If it is incorrect, write the correct punctuation on the line.

Tommy wants to go to the beach. _____

Sherry, will you give me a book to read. _____

Fred screamed, "Watch out?" _____

Will you buy me a bottle of water? _____

He shared his favorite toy with me. _____

Leave me alone. _____

Jesus tells me to love others. _____

Why do you always help others! _____

Rachel yelled, "Look out for the car." _____

Will you be in church on Sunday." _____

Write a sentence using an exclamation point.

_____

_____

Write a sentence using a question mark.

_____

_____

Holy Spirit gives _____ joy.

Apostrophes

Possessive nouns show that something is owned.
We use an apostrophe to show ownership.

Tonya's doll   Carlton's truck

Singular Possessives
When there is one owner, add an apostrophe + s. ('s)

Daddy's mug

When a singular possessive ends with s:

Proper noun: just add an (').
James'

Common noun add an ('s).
walrus's

Plural Possessives
When there is more than one owner, add an apostrophe after the s. (s')

 Turtles' shells

Underline the possessive, and write if it is singular or plural.

Maria's friend brought her two birthday gifts. _____ singular _____

The clown's makeup was melting in the sun. _____

The ants' hill was smashed by the little boy. _____

The pastor's sermon was on serving God. _____

The children's lessons made them laugh. _____

My three fish's bowls need to be cleaned. _____

The mice's trash was all over the floor. _____

Possessive Nouns

If the plural possessive doesn't end in an s,
add an apostrophe + s. ('s)

children**'s** faces

three fish**'s** worms

Write the underlined possessive correctly on the line.

We took <u>Emmas'</u> car to the grocery store. _____

The tiny <u>deers'</u> walked with their mom. _____

<u>Mrs. Peters's</u> car needs to be washed. _____

My <u>scissors'</u> blade is very sharp. _____

The <u>cows'</u> baby was running around. _____

<u>Chris's</u> favorite blanket went missing. _____

Forty <u>chef's</u> stations were ready for use. _____

<u>Marys'</u> video game needs updating. _____

Holy Spirit gives _____ peace.

Contractions

A contraction combines two words into one word.
We use an apostrophe in place of the missing letters.

I + am = I'm - Replace the (a) with an apostrophe (').

can + not = can't	does + not = doesn't	did + not = don't
are + not = aren't	have + not = haven't	is + not = isn't
do + not = don't	are+ not = aren't	
he + is = he's	she + is = she's	it + is = it's

Fill in the blank to complete the sentence.

I _____ find my favorite shoes. (can not)

My friend Stacey _____ invited me. (should have)

_____ going to play on the swings. (he is)

My mom _____ let me go to the park alone. (will not)

_____ going to help a family in need. (I am)

Write the contraction in print and cursive.

doesn't   _____

haven't   _____

More Contractions

you + **ha**ve = you've   we + **ha**ve = we've   I + **ha**ve = I've

should + **ha**ve = should've   could + **ha**ve = could've

would + **ha**ve = would've

they + **are** = they're   you + **are** = you're   we + **are** = we're

will + not = won't

Write the two words that make up each contraction.

I'm   _____   _____

she's   _____   _____

should've   _____   _____

aren't   _____   _____

could've   _____   _____

won't   _____   _____

Write the contraction for each set of words.

they are _____   can not _____

he is _____   would have _____

did not _____   you are _____

we are _____   is not _____

it is _____   I have _____

Holy Spirit gives _____ patience.

Commas

Use a comma to separate the **city and state**.
We went to visit Denver, Colorado.

Dates

Separate the day from the year with a comma.

May 1, 2025

MAY 2025						
S	M	T	W	TH	F	S
				1	2	3
4	5	6	7	8	9	10
11	12	13	14	15	16	17
18	19	20	21	22	23	24
25	26	27	28	29	30	31

Opening and Closing of a Letter

Use a comma after the greeting and closing of a letter.
Dear Mom,
 I love you! Let's talk soon.
   Sincerely,
   Ray

Rewrite the sentence and add commas where needed.

Manuel lived in Seattle Washington for six years.

_____

_____

Some scholars record the first resurrection on April 23 33 AD.

_____

_____

The zoo opened in Norfolk Virginia on March 5 1900.

_____

_____

More Commas

Use commas in **a series** to separate the items.
I bought apples, peaches, and watermelon at the store.

Transition Words
Use a comma after a transition word.

First,
Second,
Next,
Then,
Suddenly,

Connecting Sentences
Use a comma to connect two independent thoughts.

I went to the store, and I bought a football.

Put the commas where they belong in each sentence.

George bought a shirt but he decided to return it.

We used to live in Los Angeles California.

I need to buy flour oranges and chicken at the store.

First the three children went to the park.

Next we went to the bank and made a deposit.

I ate steak zucchini salad and rolls tonight.

Roger told Cathy about Jesus and she prayed to accept Jesus.

Holy Spirit gives _____ kindness.

Punctuation Letter Review

Add the punctuation to the letter.

Dear Jorge___

I___m going to tell you exciting news___ We are going to have
a party. It___s Tonya___s birthday. I am writing to invite
you___ Do you want to come___ The party will be at my
house___ I live in Memphis ___ Tennessee. We
will have games___ and we will have prizes.
There___ s going to be a lot of food. We___ re having
hotdogs___ hamburgers___ pizza___ and spaghetti___ You
don___t need to bring anything except your bathing suit. We are
going to swim in our pool. Do you know how to
swim___ I can't wait to see you at my house on
June 5___ 2025.   Sincerely___

                                             Mikey

Write the contraction in print and cursive.

should've   *should've*

_____   _____

you're   *you're*

_____   _____

Punctuation Review

Rewrite the word and add an apostrophe to show possession.

The food of the baby   _____baby's food_____

The honey of the bees   _____

The Bible of the pastor   _____

The toys of the children   _____

The cheese of the mice   _____

The favor of the Lord   _____

The waves of the ocean   _____

Write the sentence in cursive and add the correct punctuation.

He's my favorite preacher   *He's my favorite preacher.*

_____

_____

Do you like Sarah's book   *Do you like Sarah's book.*

_____

_____

Holy Spirit speaks to _____.

Abbreviating Titles

An abbreviation is a shortened way to write a word.
Put a period at the end of most abbreviations.

Mister = **Mr.**   Misses = **Mrs.**   Senior = **Sr.**   Junior = **Jr.**

Rewrite each sentence using an abbreviation
for the underlined words.

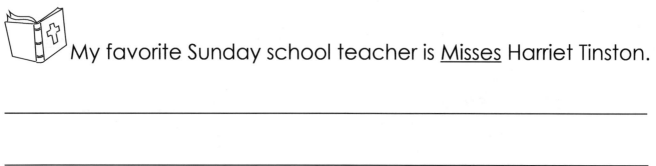 My favorite Sunday school teacher is <u>Misses</u> Harriet Tinston.

_____

_____

John Wilson <u>Senior</u> is an amazing pilot.

_____

_____

 <u>Mister</u> George Eicker teaches me how to play the guitar.

_____

_____

My friend, Calvin <u>Junior</u>, likes to jump on the trampoline.

_____

_____

More Titles

We can abbreviate positions of people.

Pastor = **Pr.**   Professor = **Prof.**   President = **Pres.**
Governor = **Gov.**   General = **Gen.**   Captain = **Capt.**

Rewrite the phrase using an abbreviation
for the underlined word.

<u>Misses</u> Wilson _____

<u>Professor</u> Blackstone _____

<u>Doctor</u> Phillips _____

<u>Pastor</u> Frank Farrell _____

Paul Quail, <u>Senior</u> _____

<u>General</u> George Washington _____

<u>President</u> John Adams _____

<u>Captain</u> Karl Branchy _____

<u>Mister</u> Tommy Smiggles _____

<u>Governor</u> William Franklin _____

Holy Spirit gives _____ goodness.

Abbreviating Days of the week

We can abbreviate the days of the week.

Monday = **Mon.**   Tuesday = **Tues.**   Wednesday = **Wed.**
Thursday = **Thurs.** Friday = **Fri.** Saturday = **Sat.** Sunday = **Sun.**

Write the abbreviation for the day that comes in between.

Monday _____ Wednesday

Friday _____ Sunday

Sunday _____ Tuesday

Wednesday _____ Friday

Saturday _____ Monday

Tuesday _____ Thursday

Thursday _____ Saturday

Write a sentence about what you do on Sunday.
Write Sunday as an abbreviation.

_____

_____

Write a sentence about what you do on Thursday.
Write Thursday as an abbreviation.

_____

_____

Days of the week

Write the day of the week and it's abbreviation

The first day of the week.

_____ Sunday _____   _____ Sun. _____

The fourth day of the week.

_____   _____

The second day of the week.

_____   _____

The fifth day of the week.

_____   _____

The day that comes before Wednesday.

_____   _____

The day that comes after Friday.

_____   _____

The day that comes after Thursday.

_____   _____

Holy Spirit gives _____ gentleness.

Abbreviating Months

We can abbreviate the months of the year.

January = **Jan.**   February = **Feb.**   March = **Mar.**
April = **Apr.**   May = **May**   June = **Jun.**

What month is it? Write the answer in abbreviation form.

I am the shortest month.	Summer officially starts this month.	April showers bring flowers this month.
_____	_____	_____
We celebrate the New Year this month.	Spring officially starts this month.	We often celebrate Jesus' resurrection this month.
_____	_____	_____

Write the month and its abbreviation in cursive.

February   *February*   *Feb.*

            _____   _____

April   *April*   *Apr.*

            _____   _____

More Months

We can abbreviate the months of the year.

July = **Jul.**   August = **Aug.**   September = **Sept.**
October = **Oct.**   November = **Nov.**   December = **Dec.**

What month is it? Write the answer in abbreviation form.

This month is in the fall and has 31 days. _____	Fall officially starts this month. _____	The United States became independent this month. _____
We celebrate the birth of Jesus in this month. _____	Thanksgiving is celebrated this month. _____	This is the last month of summer. It has 31 days. _____

Match the month to its abbreviation.

July	Aug.
August	Dec.
September	Oct.
October	Jul.
November	Sept
December	Nov.

Holy Spirit gives _____ faithfulness.

Abbreviating English Measurements

We can abbreviate liquid measurements.

teaspoon - **tsp.**   pint - **pt.**   quart - **qt.**   ounce - **oz.**
tablespoon - **tbsp.**   cup - **c.**   gallon - **gal.**   volume - **vol.**

Write the abbreviations for the measurements in the directions.

Chocolate Chip Cookies

Ingredients:

1/2 **cup** of butter
1 **cup** of sugar
1 **tablespoon** of vanilla
1 egg

1 **teaspoon** of baking powder
1/2 **teaspoon** of salt
2 **cups** of flour
12 **ounce** of chocolate chips.

Directions:

(Remember to ask an adult for help with the oven)

Preheat the oven to 350 degrees.

Cream together 1/2 _____ of butter, 1 _____ of sugar,

1 _____ of vanilla and 1 egg in a mixer until it is smooth.

In a separate bowl, mix together 2 _____ of flour,

1 _____ of baking powder, and 1/2 _____ of salt.

Mix the dry ingredients into the wet ingredients.

Add 12 _____ of chocolate chips.

Drop by the spoonful onto a cookie sheet and bake for 15 minutes.

More English Measurements

We can abbreviate solid measurements.

yard - **yd.**   foot - **ft.**   inch - **in.**   centimeter - **cm.**
mile - **mi.**   millimeter - **mm.**   meter - **m.**   pounds - **lb.**

Underline the unit of measurement, and
write its abbreviation on the line.

I ran a half-marathon that was 13.1 miles.   _____

That yard stick is 3 yards long.   _____

My shoes are 2 inches longer than his.   _____

The worm measured 10 centimeters.   _____

My dog weighs 65 pounds.   _____

My pinky nail is 12 millimeters long.   _____

There are a little over 3 feet in 1 meter.   _____

The fence around my house is 6 feet tall.   _____

Holy Spirit gives _____ self-control.

Abbreviations Review

Circle the abbreviation that is used correctly.

On Monday (Mo./Mon.) we saw a shark at the beach.

General (Gen./Gnr.) George Washington believed in prayer.

There are four quarts (qts./qrts.) in a gallon (gln./gal.).

Misses (Mrs./Ms.) Williams is a singer at our church.

The recipe calls for two teaspoons (tsp./tbsp.) of vanilla.

I need one cup (c./cp.) of almonds for my cake.

I go to my church on Wednesday (Wedn./Wed.).

We celebrate Christmas in December (Dec./Decm.).

I brought one pint (pt./pnt.) of tea to the party.

There are eight ounces (os./oz.) in a glass of water.

This November (Novem./Nov.) we are going to Canada.

We have Sunday (Sud./Sun.) dinner as a family every week.

Abbreviations Review

Match the correct word to the abbreviation.

Carl White Junior	Prof.
Governor Jackson	Mrs.
Professor Robert Oak	Pres.
Mister Larzon	Ps.
Pastor Doug Newell	Capt.
Misses Emily Grason	Gov.
President Trump	Mr.
Captain Mike Walls	Jr.

Choose the abbreviation to complete the sentence.

vol.   lbs.   yd.   in.   mi.

There are twelve _____ in a foot. (inches)

The baby weighed six _____ at birth. (pounds)

I ran a_____ in my school's track meet. (mile)

We measured the_____ of the liquid in a beaker. (volume)

I need a _____ of materials to make my dress. (yard)

_____ has God's favor.

Nouns and Adjectives

A **noun** is a person, place, thing, or idea.

Person	Place	Thing	Idea
Matt	Egypt	sailboat	faith

Adjectives tell about nouns. Questions they answer:

What color?	What kind?	What size?	How many?

How does it look?   How does it taste?   How does it feel?

How does it behave?   What shape?   How does it smell?

My <u>hungry</u> dog looked at the <u>blue</u> bowl as he waited for food.

How does my dog feel? **hungry**   What color bowl? **blue**

Which question does the underlines adjective answer?

My brother's blanket is <u>soft</u>. _____

I dipped the <u>sweet</u> carrot in ranch. _____

I bought a <u>large</u> orange juice. _____

The <u>cute</u> mouse ate the cheese. _____

My dog watched the <u>angry</u> bird. _____

The <u>circular</u> driveway is long._____

Take out the <u>stinky</u> garbage._____

Adjectives

Underline the adjective in each sentence.

Esther was given a beautiful crown and jewels as queen.

David fought Goliath with five stones.

Jonah was swallowed by a huge whale.

Moses saw a burning bush and heard God's voice.

Abraham left all of his loving family to follow God.

David played beautiful music for King Saul.

Jacob gave Joseph a colorful coat.

David took off his royal robe to dance before the Lord.

Jesus died on a wood cross for our sins.

Write a sentence using the adjective: three.

_____

_____

Write a sentence using the adjective: salty.

_____

_____

_____ cannot fail with Jesus.

Articles

Articles are words that come before a noun.
A, **an**, and **the** are articles.

a pony   an otter   the ostrich

Use (**an**) in front of a word that starts with a (short) vowel sound.
Use (**a**) in front of a word that starts with a (long vowel) consonant sound.

a unicycle   **an** umbrella   **an** hour   **a** hat

Circle the correct article.

Jesse found (a / an) purple stone.

Gerri saw (a / an) comet in the night sky.

We saw (an / the) tiger crossing the road.

In August we sang (a / an) song at church.

My soccer coach gave me (a / an) uniform.

God created (an / the) universe.

I saw (an / the) moon and stars last night.

I fed (a / an) elephant at the zoo.

My mom said to meet her in (a / an) hour.

Nouns, Adjectives, and Articles

Write the article that goes before the word.

a   an

_____ garage   _____ apple   _____ unit

_____ eagle   _____ bicycle   _____ boat

_____ fish   _____ giraffe   _____ alligator

_____ icycle   _____ kangaroo   _____ igloo

Write an adjective to describe the noun.

_____ girl   _____ butterfly

_____ stones   _____ car

_____ cake   _____ shoes

_____ church   _____ tree

Highlight the nouns and underline the adjectives.

We watched the new movie on our blue iPad.

My best friend told me a funny joke that made me laugh.

The little girl told her brother that she wanted a chewy cookie.

The handsome farmer is growing tall trees.

I like to make cute t-shirts to sell on my computer.

Jesus loves _____.

Verbs and Adverbs

A **verb** is an action word.

run	jump	swim	hike

Adverbs describe verbs, adjectives, and other adverbs.
Questions they answer:

How?   To what extent?   When?   Where?

verbs	**adjectives**	**adverbs**
He <u>selfishly</u> refused to share his candy.	He was really sweet to me <u>today</u>.	Tina slept <u>very</u> early.
How did he refuse?	When?	To what extent?
selfishly	today	very

What question does the underlined adverb answer?

Jesus stays with us <u>everywhere</u>. _____

Jesus knows us <u>so</u> well. _____

Kimmy slept <u>peacefully</u>. _____

I <u>always</u> pray to Jesus. _____

Sammy jumped <u>happily</u>. _____

Adverbs
Many adverbs end in ly: really, surprisingly, quickly

Some words that end in **ly** are <u>not</u> adverbs	Many adverbs do <u>not</u> end in **ly**
Verbs	**To What Extent?**
multiply reply apply	always often never
Adjectives	**When?**
lovely friendly	after before
Nouns	**Where?**
family jelly firefly	here outside near

Underline the adverb in each sentence.

I always like to multiply the numbers in my math book.

Before you sit down, please give me my iPad.

Do you want to eat dinner now?

I carefully cut out the star for our poster today.

I call my friend every day and ask him to play.

George excitedly told his mom about his new medal.

My family often visits the nursing home to bless others.

I gently placed the necklace on the dresser.

_____ is a child of God.

Nouns, Adjectives, Verbs, and Adverbs

Is the underlined word a noun, adjective, verb, or adverbs?

Frank wants to go to <u>Miami</u> with his favorite cousin Wyatt.

noun   adjective   verb   adverb

She <u>quietly</u> told her father about her day.

noun   adjective   verb   adverb

Jesus <u>healed</u> everyone who was sick and oppressed.

noun   adjective   verb   adverb

The sparkling water was bottled from a <u>fresh</u> spring.

noun   adjective   verb   adverb

The Bible says that Jesus came to give us <u>abundant</u> life.

noun   adjective   verb   adverb

Deedee found her kitten under the bed <u>today</u>.

noun   adjective   verb   adverb

We want to <u>apply</u> this money to our bill.

noun   adjective   verb   adverb

Nouns and Adjectives

Writing with parts of speech.
Choose a noun and an adjective from the
word boxes to write five sentences.

Nouns			Adjectives		
kangaroo	clock	boy	tasty	mini	fancy
cupcake	airplane	store	super	huge	wonderful
computer	wires	girl	giant	lovely	enjoyable
truck	shoes	pillow	kind	happy	excellent

_____

_____

_____

_____

_____

_____

_____

_____

_____

_____

God helps _____ to succeed.

A Silly Day with My Cousin

Write a word for each part of speech without reading the story.
Then, read the silly story.

Today I went on a play date with my cousin Mark. We spent the

_____ day together. First, we went to a restaurant
(adjective)

for _____. We _____ ate eggs, bacon,
(noun)   (adverb)

and fruit. We drank hot chocolate. Our waiter was_____
(adverb)

funny. Then, we went to the park. We _____ on the
(verb)

playground. We played Frisbee. We fed the squirrel yummy

_____. One squirrel _____ tried to climb
(noun)   (adverb)

up my leg! When we left the park we _____ to the
(verb)

mall. We made stuffed animals. I made a_____
(noun)

Mark made a walrus. Finally, we went to Wendy's for lunch. I

_____ a fried chicken sandwich. I ate fries with a
(verb)

_____ cheese sauce. I laughed when Mark used
(adjective)

his _____ to look like a walrus. We decided to
(noun)

plan another play date while we_____.
(verb)

Verbs and Adverbs

Writing with parts of speech.
Choose a verb and an adverb from the
word boxes to write five sentences.

Verbs			Adverbs		
whisper	arrive	pack	easily	sometimes	loudly
remove	give	enjoy	twice	playfully	silently
bake	follow	love	daily	nearby	soon
open	paint	shop	well	once	very

_____

_____

_____

_____

_____

_____

_____

_____

_____

Week 28 _____ is strong in the Lord.

Simple Subjects and Predicates

Simple **Subject**	Simple **Predicate**
The simple subject is the noun (person, place, or thing) the sentence is about.	The simple predicate is the verb that tells about the subject.
Tom	cries

When we combine the simple subject and the simple predicate, we get a simple sentence.

Tom cries.

Is the underlined word the subject or the predicate?

<u>Wanda</u> ran.   _____

<u>God</u> created.   _____

Sandra <u>followed</u>.   _____

<u>Carson</u> spoke.   _____

<u>Jesus</u> saves.   _____

Herbert <u>eats</u>.   _____

Jenny <u>prayed</u>.   _____

Subjects and Predicates

Underline the simple subject (noun) in each sentence.

Callie winked.

Abbie dances.

Ryan preached.

George drives.

Tim reads.

Izzy asked.

Jimena walks.

Barbara forgot.

Carla calls.

Debbie yelled.

Eli slept.

Jose borrowed.

Underline the simple predicate (verb) in each sentence.

Donnie catches.

Zoe cooks.

Maelin enjoys.

Luis found.

Kris flew.

Nellie gave.

Oliver cleans.

Penelope arrived.

Quinton responded.

Rachel Climbs.

Sammy collects.

Miguel slipped.

_____ trusts in God.

Writing Simple Parts of Speech

Add a subject (noun) to each sentence.

_____ played.

_____ danced.

_____ wept.

_____ sings.

_____ worshiped.

_____ drives.

Add a predicate (verb) to each sentence.

Rebekah _____.

Edgar _____.

Miriam _____.

David _____.

Naomi _____.

Ruth _____.

More Simple Parts of Speech

If the sentence is missing a subject, write subject on the line.
If the sentence is missing a predicate, write predicate on the line.

_____ dances in worship.   _____

My friend Rachel _____.   _____

Trace, the singer, _____.   _____

_____ walks to the store.   _____

_____ gives presents.   _____

_____ swims at the beach. _____

Delilah _____.   _____

_____ shopped for cupcakes. _____

The gymnast_____.   _____

Sam and Terrance _____. _____

_____ saw a shark.   _____

General Zadai _____.   _____

God watches over _____.

Complete Subjects and Predicates

Complete **Subject**	Complete **Predicate**
The complete subject is <u>all the words</u> that tell about the subject (noun).	The complete predicate is <u>all the words</u> that tell about the predicate (verb).
My dad's friend Tom	**cried during the movie.**

We combine the complete subject and the complete predicate to get a complete sentence.

 My dad's friend Tom cried during the movie.

Are the underlined words the complete subject or predicate?

Shawn <u>went to a soccer game</u>. _____

My little sister painted a picture for me. _____

Frankie scored the first point. _____

The black marker <u>fell off the desk</u>. _____

My puppy <u>ran into the street</u>. _____

I <u>know how to play Uno</u>. _____

Cliff can ride a unicycle without falling. _____

The black and white zebra ran away. _____

Subjects and Predicates

Underline the complete subject in each sentence.

The Lord God said that He would flood the earth.

God told Noah to build an ark.

Noah's three sons helped him build the ark.

When the time was right, God sent the animals to the ark.

The animals came two by two.

The flood destroyed everything.

A rainbow appeared in the sky as a promise.

Underline the complete predicate in each sentence.

Joseph was the son of Jacob and Rachel.

Jacob loved his son very much.

A coat of many colors was given to Joseph as a gift.

Joseph's brothers sold him to be a slave in Egypt.

The favor of the Lord rested upon Joseph.

Pharaoh had a dream that only Joseph could interpret.

Joseph became a mighty leader in Egypt.

_____ seeks God.

Writing complete Subjects and Predicates

Add a complete subject to each sentence.

_____ listened to the Lord.

_____ wrote a book.

_____ talks about Jesus.

_____ loves Jesus.

_____ spoke to an angel.

_____ killed a giant.

Add a complete subject to each sentence.

The Apostle Paul _____.

King David _____.

My friend Wilbur_____.

Naomi's daughter _____.

TeShawn's mom _____.

The three Hebrew boys _____.

Subject and Predicate Review

Underline the **simple** subject.
Change the sentence by rewriting the **complete** subject.

My sweet pony Percy loves to eat crunchy apples and carrots.

_____

_____

The young pastor told people about Jesus everywhere he went.

_____

_____

The whole church gathered to worship Jesus.

_____

_____

The brave knight decided to stay and fight for the Lord.

_____

_____

My precious baby sister Tammy cries when she is hungry.

_____

_____

_____ shows the love of Jesus.

Complete Subjects and Predicates

Underline the complete subject and highlight
the complete predicate.

Jonah was a prophet of the Lord.

One day God told Jonah to go to Nineveh.

The people of Nineveh were very evil.

Prophet Jonah did not want to go.

He boarded a ship going in the opposite direction.

A bad storm came against the ship.

The wooden ship started to sink.

All of the workers threw things off the ship.

Disobedient Jonah was asleep in the ship.

The captain woke Jonah up.

The terrible storm would stop when they threw Jonah overboard.

A huge fish swallowed Jonah.

Jonah was in the fish for three days.

The fish spit Jonah out.

The people of Nineveh heard the message and repented.

Subject and Predicate Review

Underline the **simple** predicate.
Tell what else the Bible character did by
rewriting the **complete** predicate.

The shepherd boy, David, took care of his father's sheep.

_____

_____

Beautiful Queen Esther fasted and prayed before the Lord.

_____

_____

The Apostle Paul wrote letters to the churches.

_____

_____

Jesus' parents, Joseph and Mary, took Jesus to Egypt.

_____

_____

Faithful Noah built an ark according to God's directions.

_____

_____

God strengthens _____.

Diagramming Sentences

Diagramming sentences helps the reader identify the connections between different parts of a sentence.

These are the parts of speech we have learned so far:

Noun   Verb   Adjective   Adverb   Article

The main part of the sentence, subject and predicate, go on the base line. We separate them with a vertical predicate line.

Wesley preaches.

predicate line

subject (noun)   predicate (verb)

Wesley   preaches

base line ➡

(Who or what the sentence is about.)   (Tells the action to the subject)

Label the parts of this diagram like the one above.

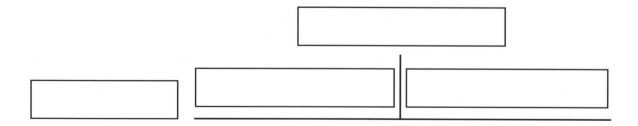

Fill in the diagram by writing the subject and the predicate on the base line.

Robert swings.

Diagramming Simple Sentences

Draw the vertical predicate line. Then write the simple subject and predicate.

Mr. Snowman melted.

_____

Kevin gave.

_____

Governor Randolph served.

_____

People clapped.

_____

Grace Ann flew.

_____

Allen played.

_____

God upholds _____ with His right hand.

Diagramming with Adjectives

We can diagram other parts of speech besides the subject and predicate. To diagram an adjective and article, write them on the diagonal lines underneath the base line on the subject side.

predicate line

subject (noun)   predicate (verb)

base line ➤

article   adjective

An adjective describes a noun.

The tiny chicks peeped.

The word **tiny** is an adjective that describes the chicks. It tells their size.

Diagram the adjective like this:

chicks | peeped

The   tiny

Label the parts of this diagram like the one above.

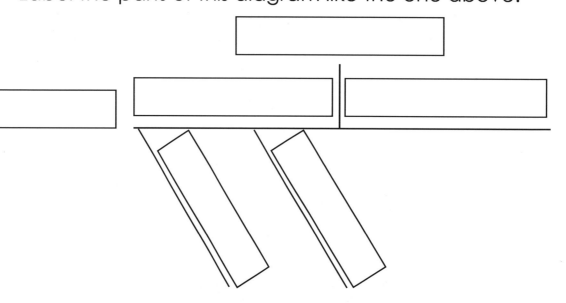

Diagramming Sentences

Trace the lines for the diagram. Fill in the diagram by writing the subject and predicate. Then write the adjective and article.

A pretty snowflake melted.

The sweet lady cooked.

A happy walrus smiled.

An educated man taught.

The perfect cake tipped.

An orange tiger growled.

God has a plan for _____.

Diagramming with Adverbs

We can diagram other parts of speech besides the subject, predicate, and adjectives. To diagram an adverb, write it on a diagonal line underneath the base line on the predicate side.

predicate line

subject (noun)   predicate (verb)

base line ➡

adverb

An adverb describes a verb, adjective, or adverb.

Mary swung happily.

The word **happily** is an adjective that describes Mary's action. It tells how she swung.

Diagram the adverb like this:

Mary | swung

happily

Label the parts of the diagram like the one above.

Diagramming Sentences

Trace the lines for the diagram. Fill in the diagram by writing the subject and predicate. Then write the adverb.

Pastor preached lovingly.

Miguel laughed a lot.

Isa jumps always.

Lions hunt swiftly.

Bears growl wildly.

Puppies bark constantly.

_____ is known by God.

Diagramming with Adjectives and Adverbs

Many sentences have both adjectives and adverbs.
A diagram with both parts of speech looks like this:

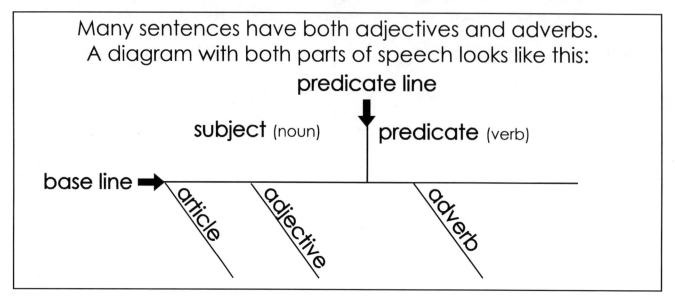

The brown eagle sat still.

The word **brown** describes the eagle. The word **still** describes how the eagle sat.

Diagram the adverb and adjective like this:

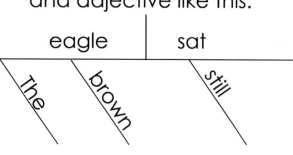

Label the parts of the diagram like the one above.

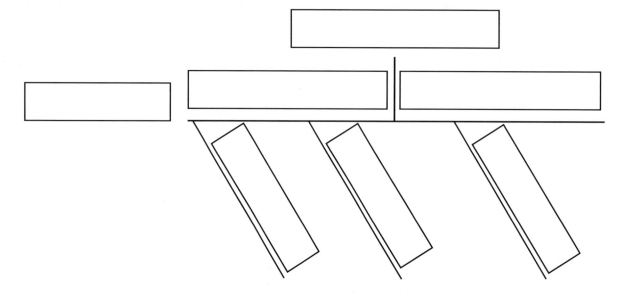

Diagramming Complete Sentences

Trace the lines for the diagram. Then write the subject, predicate, article, adjective, and adverb.

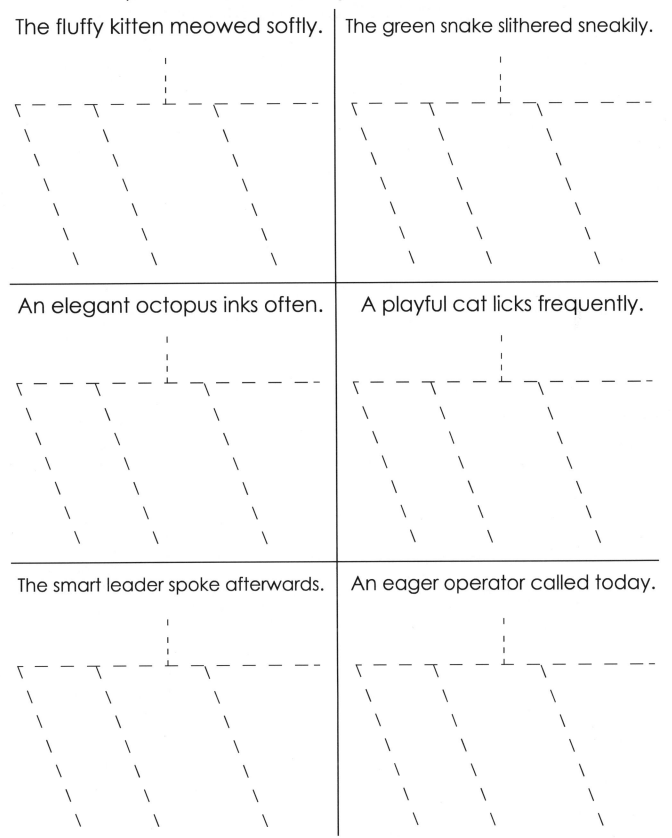

The fluffy kitten meowed softly.

The green snake slithered sneakily.

An elegant octopus inks often.

A playful cat licks frequently.

The smart leader spoke afterwards.

An eager operator called today.

Diagramming Sentences

Fill in the diagram for each sentence.

People talk excitedly.

The crazy clown danced.

A blue sailboat sailed.

The nice artist painted beautifully.

The pretty singer sings professionally.

Actors sobbed successfully.

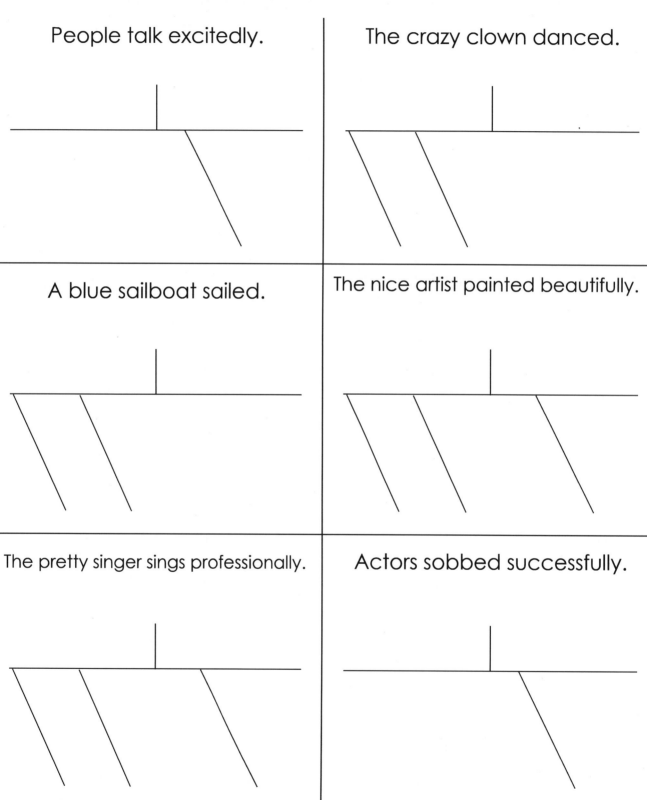

Diagramming Sentences

Draw and fill in the diagram for each sentence.

Blaire smiled.

The funny captain joked.

Audiences applauded wildly.

A sporty car raced madly.

The colorful fish swam freely.

The praying girl heard clearly.

_____ walks in God's favor.

Punctuation Review

Write a comma where it belongs in each sentence.

I was born on October 23 2015.

Our vacation started in Austin Texas and ended in Florida.

Suddenly the sky turned dark and rain began to pour down.

I went to a play and they handed out programs.

Will you buy spinach carrots and olives at the store?

Rewrite these phrases using an apostrophe to show possession.

gifts of the Holy Spirit _____ Holy Spirit's gifts _____

leaves of the trees _____

paint of the painter _____

jewelry of the woman _____

cocoon of the caterpillar _____

Word of God _____

wings of the birds _____

Transformation

Write in the missing punctuation (commas, end marks, and apostrophes) in the story below. There are 16 mistakes.

Kipper the caterpillar had a cozy life He spent his days crawling from leaf to leaf. He had a lot of friends They spent their days laughing talking and eating. They traveled together and they had so much fun. One day kipper found himself all alone. Where had his friends gone Kipper was sad. He looked for them but all he could find were strange lumps of spun silk. Kipper ate a quick meal. He spun a silk blanket around himself. He fell asleep feeling sorry for himself. Kipper woke up in a dark place. He didnt know what was happening but he knew that he was changing. He knew that the Creator was making him into something new He was in the dark place for ten days and then something happened. Kipper realized that he had wings He pushed against the blanket until he was wrapped in the suns bright light. Kipper used his wings to fly high into the sky. Thats when he saw his friends. They were flying too He joined them as they soared into the sky. No longer did they stay near the ground moving from leaf to leaf. They were able to soar into the sky. God had done a great work in them

_____ shows God's love to others.

Abbreviations Review

Match the word to its abbreviation.

Mister		Dec.
Monday		Jr.
March		Mrs.
yard		Wed.
cup		c.
Misses		Prof.
October		Mr.
Wednesday		Mon.
Junior		in.
Professor		Mar.
December		yd.
inches		Oct.

More Abbreviations

Write the word that goes with the abbreviation.

cm. _____

Sr. _____

mi. _____

Pres. _____

Apr. _____

tbsp. _____

Capt. _____

Sat. _____

mm. _____

Gov. _____

Fri. _____

lb. _____

tsp. _____

Jan. _____

Thurs. _____

pt. _____

God loves _____.

Parts of Speech Review

Decide if the underlined word is an adjective
or adverb, and write it on the line.

Destiny rode her bike <u>everyday</u> for a month. _____

My beautiful friend gave me <u>three</u> gifts. _____

We played in the leaves <u>today</u>. _____

A <u>sweet</u> kitten meowed at my feet. _____

The <u>loving</u> preacher told me about Jesus. _____

Our <u>spinning</u> planet is God's creation. _____

The faithful servant served <u>lovingly</u>. _____

The <u>crying</u> toddler wanted a puppy. _____

The bright light went out <u>quickly</u>. _____

The ferocious lion roared <u>loudly</u>. _____

Jesus healed all people <u>willingly</u>. _____

Adjectives and Adverb Review

Circle the adjective, and underline the noun it tells about.

A rough fisherman was cleaning his nets.

Peaceful Jesus climbed into Peter's boat.

Jesus wanted to talk the huge crowd from the boat.

Peter let Jesus use his wooden boat to teach.

Jesus taught the eager crowd.

Jesus told Peter to take his boat to deep water.

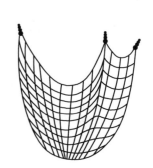

Jesus said that Peter would have a great catch.

Peter told Jesus that his empty nets meant there were no fish.

Circle the adverb, and underline the noun,
verb or adjective it tells about.

Peter said he would follow Jesus obediently.

Peter quickly went out to the deep water.

He threw his empty nets into the water once.

The nets began to collect fish rapidly.

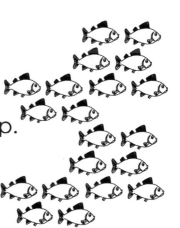

Peter hurriedly cried out to his partners for help.

Both boats were completely filled.

Peter left everything to follow Jesus.

_____ is a child of God.

Subjects and Predicates Review

Highlight the simple subject and underline the simple predicate.

The Israelites lived in Egypt safely.

A mean Pharaoh made the Israelites slaves.

The sad Israelites cried out to God.

The weary people asked God to help them.

Almighty God sent a baby.

Pharaoh decided that all baby boys must die.

One brave woman hid her baby.

The smart mother placed him in a basket.

The little basket was placed in the river.

Her sweet daughter watched over the basket.

The royal princess found the baby.

She called him Moses.

The happy woman adopted Moses.

More Subjects and Predicates

Read the simple subject and finish the
sentence by writing a complete predicate.

The beautiful butterfly _____

_____

The annoying fly _____

_____

The crazy squirrel _____

_____

The smelly skunks _____

_____

The tall giraffes _____

_____

The playful monkeys _____

_____

The intelligent puppy _____

_____

God's plans are for_____'s good.

Diagramming Sentences Review

Fill in the diagram for each sentence.

Jesus taught lovingly.

The sweet lady prayed.

A loud timer beeped.

An orange cat ran inside.

The kind preacher gave generously.

Birds fly often.

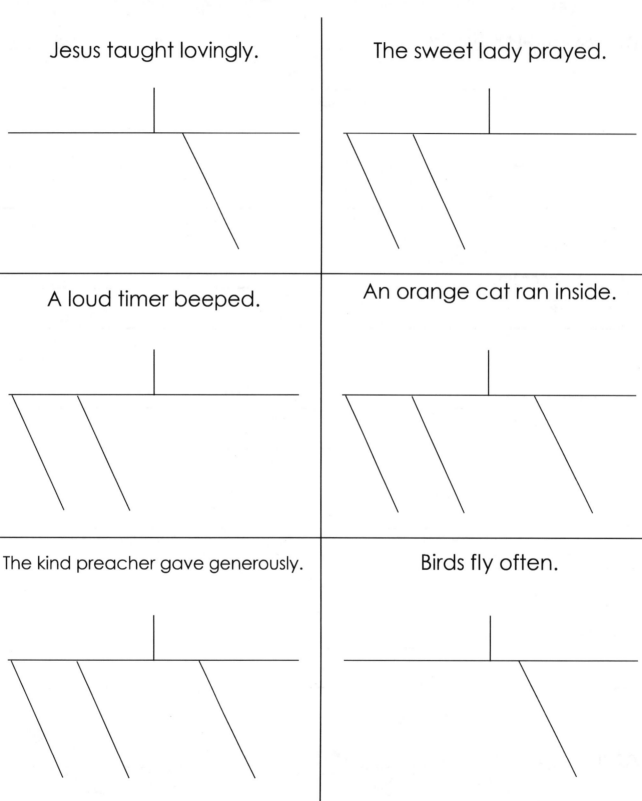

Diagramming Sentences

Draw and fill in the diagram for each sentence.

Jesus saves.

A perfect teacher taught.

Children played loudly.

The fine musician played easily.

Write a sentence and then diagram it.

Unit 6
Week 31-36

Writing

Unit 6 Instructions

This unit focuses on writing. Your child will be learning about and practicing various types of writing. Excellent readers make excellent writers. While this unit focuses on writing, it is important to continue reading. Reading provides your child with examples of exceptional writing from published authors.

The first two weeks of the unit give your child a chance to recognize different genres of writing. It is recommended that you provide a variety of books for extended practice. One suggestion would be to go to the library and check out fiction, nonfiction, and poetry books. The daily lessons can be extended by previewing and reading the genre that is being worked on that day.

The last four weeks provide extensive writing practice. These weeks take your child through the writing process. It is important that each step is followed. There are no shortcuts to excellent writing. Drafting is just as important as publishing. When your child begins revising and editing be sure to explain the difference. Revising is working on word choice and placement. This is where words are taken away and added. Editing is working with the mechanics of writing. Here your child will work with spelling, punctuation, capitalization, and spacing. A good practice to teach and continue is to have your child write on every other line. This gives the writer an opportunity to make changes on the spaces in between each line.

It is recommended that your child read a book of choice for thirty minutes a day. The more reading practice, the better the reader. Reading together is a great way to allow your child to practice while still being able to provide support!

Week 31

Opinion Writing

An opinion is the way a person believes, thinks, or feel, about a subject.

There are **four steps** to follow when writing an opinion piece:

1st: Opinion	2nd: Reason	3rd: Examples	4th: Opinion
Tell your reader **how** you feel about the subject.	Tell your reader **why** you feel that way about the subject.	Give your reader 2-3 **examples** for why you feel that way.	**Restate** your opinion for your reader.

1st: There are many ways to start an opinion writing. Here are a few examples:

In my opinion...   I think...   I feel...

I believe...   I know...   Everyone should...

What is your opinion?:
I think that strawberry ice cream is the best ice cream.

2nd: Why do you believe that way?:
I believe that strawberry ice cream is the best because it is my favorite flavor.

3rd: Example 1

Strawberry ice cream has real strawberries in it.

Example 2

Ice cream with fresh fruit is healthy.

4th: What is your opinion?:
I think that strawberry ice cream is the best ice cream.

Opinion Writing

Circle **Yes** or **No** for each statement.

I know that I take good care of my pets.	Yes	No
I think that ice cream is the best snack.	Yes	No
I feel like kids should have more time to play.	Yes	No
In my opinion, birthday parties are fun.	Yes	No
Everyone should have a family pet.	Yes	No

Choose one statement that you circled yes. Make a plan for writing about it by filling out this graphic organizer.

What is your opinion?

_____

_____

Why do you believe that way?

_____

_____

Example 1:

_____

_____

_____

_____

_____

Example 2:

_____

_____

_____

_____

_____

What is your opinion?

_____

_____

_____ is special to God.

Persuasive Writing

Persuasive writing is written to convince the reader to agree with the author. It uses your opinion to influence others.

There are **four steps** to follow when writing a persuasive piece:

1st: Belief	2nd: Point	3rd: Reasons	4th: Belief
Tell the belief you want your reader to **agree with**.	Share at least **2 points** with your reader for your belief.	Give 1-3 reasons **why** your reader should agree with your point.	**Restate** what you want your reader to agree with.

1st: A few sentence starters for persuasive writing are...

We all know that _____. Most people would agree that _____.

I strongly believe _____. It is really important that _____.

What belief do you want your reader to agree with?:
I strongly believe that I should get a new bike.

2nd: **Point 1**

My bike is too small for me to ride.

3rd: **Reason 1**

I have grown taller.

Reason 2

I don't need training wheels anymore.

Point 2

I can share my old bike with another kid.

Reason 1

I took care of my bike and it looks like new.

Reason 2

Many kids don't have a bike of their own.

4th: What is your belief?
I strongly believe that I should get a new bike.

Persuasive Writing

Circle **Yes** or **No** for each statement.

My parents should let me have more than one pet.   Yes   No

All kids should get to go to an amusement park.   Yes   No

We all know that kids need a lot of time to play.   Yes   No

All kids should share their toys.   Yes   No

Choose one statement that you circled yes. Make a plan for writing about it by filling out this graphic organizer.

What is your belief?

_____

_____

Point 1: _____   Point 2: _____

_____   _____

_____   _____

_____   _____

Reason 1:   Reason 1:

_____   _____

_____   _____

_____   _____

Reason 2:   Reason 2:

_____   _____

_____   _____

_____   _____

What is your belief?

_____

_____

Jesus is a friend to _____.

Informative Writing

Informative writing is written to tell a reader about a specific subject. It does not try to convince a reader. It includes: facts, details, and explanations.
Examples: reports, articles, how-to, invitations, recipes

There are **four steps** to follow when writing an informative piece:

| 1st: Topic Choose a **topic** you want to talk about. | 2nd: Topic Sentence Write a **topic sentence** that tells what your topic is. | 3rd: Facts Write at least 3 **facts**. | 4th: Conclusion Write a sentence that **sums it up**. |

1st: **Topic**

How to play freeze tag.

2nd: **Topic Sentence**

Here are some ways to begin an informative writing.

Let me tell you about ____. I know many things about ___.

I can describe ____.   I can teach you about ____.

Let me tell you about how to play Freeze Tag.

3rd: **Facts**

| Fact 1: One person is chosen to be it.  | Fact 2: The person who is it chases people and tags them. They have to freeze. | Fact 3: You can only unfreeze if another person tags you. |

4th: **Conclusion** Sentence

As you can see, I know a lot about how to play Freeze Tag.

Informative Writing

Circle **Yes** or **No** for each statement.

I know information about animals.	Yes	No
I know information about a sport.	Yes	No
I know information about rainbows.	Yes	No
I know information about how to cook.	Yes	No
I know information about how to play a game.	Yes	No

Choose one statement that you circled yes. Make a plan for writing about it by filling out this graphic organizer.

Topic: _____

_____

Topic Sentence: _____

_____

Fact 1:	Fact 2:	Fact 3:
_____	_____	_____
_____	_____	_____
_____	_____	_____
_____	_____	_____
_____	_____	_____
_____	_____	_____
_____	_____	_____

Conclusion Sentence: _____

_____

_____

_____ loves Jesus.

Narrative Writing

Narrative writing tells a story.

Personal Narrative:	**Fictional Narrative:**
...is a story that happened to you.	...is a make-believe story (not true).
...is based on true events.	...is written like a story.
...shows feelings and emotion.	...shows the feelings of the characters.

Narrative Writing has:

- Beginning, Middle, and End   - Characters

- Problem and a Solution   - Setting

Who are the characters?	Where and when does the story take place?	How does the story start?
Sally	When Sally was eight.	Sally goes to an amusement park for her birthday.
Dad		

What are the main events? (What is going to happen?)

Sally goes to Milky Way Park for her birthday.

She goes with her family.

Sally's dad wants her to go on a roller coaster.

Sally is scared.

Sally's dad promises to go with her.

How will your story end?

Sally goes on the roller coaster with her dad and ends up loving it. She is not afraid.

Narrative Writing

Make a plan for narrative writing by filling
out this graphic organizer.

Who are the characters?

Where and when does the
story take place?

_____   _____

_____   _____

_____   _____

_____   _____

_____   _____

How does the story start?

_____

_____

_____

What are the main events?

_____

_____

_____

How will your story end?

_____

_____

_____

Types of Writing Review

Read the paragraphs below. Write down the type of writing.

Opinion   Persuasive   Informative   Narrative

Let me tell you about the ways color can be added to a drawing. One way to add color is to use pastels. Pastels make your picture look like a chalk drawing. Another way to add color is paint. Paint is pretty but can be messy. Finally, you can use markers or crayons. Many people like to use these art supplies. There are many ways to add color to a drawing.

_____

Everyone would agree that a family should have a dog. Dogs provide safety. When a family has a dog, no one is going to break in. Dogs also help kids learn to be responsible. A dog has to be walked, fed, and cleaned up after. Our family definitely needs a dog.

_____

I know that I am a wonderful person. I know this because the Bible says it. The Bible says that I am fearful and wonderfully made. I also know that I am wonderful because I am made new. When I asked Jesus to be my Savior, He made me new. I am a wonderful person.

_____

Danny always wanted to have a shiny red bicycle. He knew that his family could not afford to buy one. Danny found people in his neighborhood who paid him to do jobs. It took him six months to save enough money. Then, he heard about a family who lost everything in a fire. Danny decided to give his money to them. They were so grateful and Danny was full of joy. Two days later, Danny received a gift. It was a brand new red bicycle!

_____

More Review

I think that monkeys are the best animals for pets. First, they are very smart. Monkeys are able to be service animals. They help people by getting things for them when they are not able to get up. Second, monkeys are funny. They do all kinds of tricks and make people laugh. I think Monkeys are the perfect pets.

_____

Stan was nine when he flew on an airplane for the first time. He was very nervous. He had to fly by himself. Stan met a nice flight attendant named Kevin. Kevin helped Stan feel safe. Stan got to eat peanuts and drink soda. When the flight ended, Stan realized that God had sent someone to help him not fear anymore.

_____

I am going to tell you about Jesus. Jesus is the Son of God. He came to earth to die for all people. Jesus is the Son of Man. He lived on the earth and did many miracles. Jesus died on a cross and rose again three days later. Now Jesus lives in Heaven with His Father.

_____

You definitely need to go to Warrior Jet School. They have the best time. First, all the kids who go get to fly an airplane. It's like playing a video game, but you get to earn real points. You also get to shoot Nerf guns at the enemy. This is fun because it reminds kids that the enemy always loses! Every kid should go to Warrior Jet School!

_____

Week 32

God is speaking to _____.

Color and Sensory Poems

Poetry is writing that creates feelings or emotions.	
Color Poems Poems that uses the senses to describe one color.	**Sensory Poems** Poems that use all five senses to describe a feeling or thing.

Poetry elements you might see in these poems:

Line	Stanzas	Sensory Details
Words grouped together in one line in a poem.	Lines in a poem that are grouped together.	Using your senses to help your reader see.

Read the poems and answer the questions.

The Color Red

Red reminds me of love.
Red smells like cinnamon.
Red tastes like crisp apples.
Red looks like candy cane stripes.
Red feels like kindness.
Red is _____

How would you finish the poem?

_____

Draw a picture to go with the color poem.

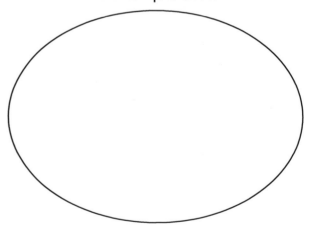

What am I?

I hear a simple song.
I smell rain in the air.
I see trees sway in the wind.
I feel soft feathers.
I taste fresh worms for lunch.

What is the sensory poem about?

_____

_____

Acrostic and Shape Poems

Acrostic Poems	Shape Poems
The first letter of each word spells out a word vertically.	Poems that are written in the shape they describe.

Read the poems and answer the questions.

A Friendly Whale

Doesn't swim alone
Outgoing
Loves fish
Playful
Has a fin
Is not a shark
Never hurts humans

What word does this

acrostic spell?

_____

What is one fact you

could add?

_____

_____

Gus loves bones. Eats these anytime. Hides them in the yard. Barkes a lot. Will do tricks for a tasty treat.

What type of poem is this?

_____

Write three words from the poem that tell you why this shape was chosen.

_____

_____

_____

Finish this acrostic poem.

bushy tail

usually eating grass

never sits too long

n_____

yard visitor

Jesus is watching over _____.

Cinquain and Haiku Poems

Cinquain Poems	Haiku Poems
A poem with five lines. Each line has a different number of syllables and part of speech.	Poems that have three lines. The lines have a specific number of syllables each.

Poetry elements you might see in these poems:

Line	Line Break	Rhythm
Words grouped together in one line in a poem.	When a line ends and the reader pauses.	The pattern of the beat in a poem.

Read the poems and answer the questions.

Cinquain Poem

Beach
Sandy, Salty
Swimming, Throwing, Building
A time to relax
Sea

How many -ing verbs are in the poem?

_____

What is the topic of the poem?

_____

What is one adjective?

_____

Haiku Poem

Lays eggs in the sand
Follows the moon to the sea
Swims in the ocean

What is the haiku about?

_____

How many syllables are in the second line?

_____

What is one action the poem talks about?

_____

Rhyming Poems

Rhyming Poems
Poems that have rhyming words, usually at the end of a line.

Poetry elements you might see in these poems:

Line	Repetition	Rhyme
Words grouped together in one line in a poem.	When a line is repeated.	Words in a poem that end with the same sound.

Read the poem and answer the questions.

Sally took a little test.
She prayed and then she did her best.
The teacher said the test was done.
Now Sally knows with God she won.
Sally took a little test.
She prayed and then she did her best.
Which words rhyme:

_____ and _____
_____ and _____

What did Sally do to help her with test?
_____
_____

Highlight the lines that show repetition.

Finish the poem by adding your own line.
Ryan wants to go to the mall.
But first he has to clean the stall.
His horse is a lot of fun.

_____
_____

Which word rhymes with mall? _____

Does this poem have repetition? _____
_____

_____ is creative.

Types of Nonfiction Writing

Nonfiction writing is writing that is true. It is based on facts.

Letters
- writing that is sent from one person to another

Informational Text	Diaries/Journals	Essays/Articles
- articles - directions - textbooks	- writings about an author's day - includes thoughts and feelings	- writings about a specific topic - written to inform, persuade, or explain

Biography
- facts written about a person's life

Autobiography
- facts written about your own life.

Write the type of nonfiction that goes with each sentence.

Today I went to a party. It made me feel happy. _____

First, make sure that you have all the clues. _____

George Washington was the first president. _____

I believe that every child should have a pet. _____

Dear Jane, thank you for the lovely gift. _____

I am a student who works hard. _____

Let me tell you all about the first car. _____

Nonfiction

Write the type of nonfiction on the line under the book.

Autobiography	Information Text	Diary/Journal
Essay/Articles	Biography	Letter

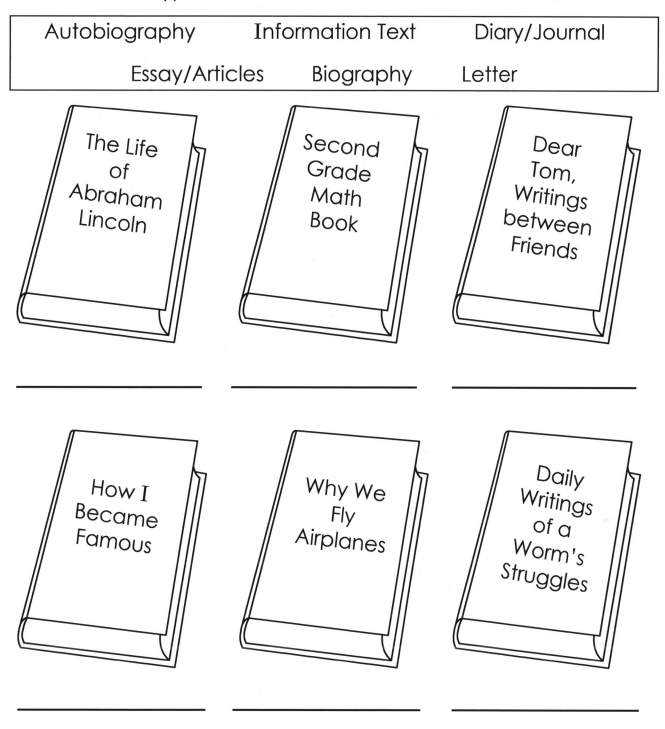

The Life of Abraham Lincoln

Second Grade Math Book

Dear Tom, Writings between Friends

_____

How I Became Famous

Why We Fly Airplanes

Daily Writings of a Worm's Struggles

_____

What type of nonfiction do you write about yourself?

_____
_____

_____ believes God's Word.

Types of Fiction Writing

Fiction writing is writing that is make-believe.

Historical Fiction	Realistic Fiction	Fantasy
A story that takes place in the past.	A story that is not true, but could be true.	A story that has impossible elements such as talking animals.

Folktales	Mystery	Adventure
A story that is told from one generation to the next.	A story that has clues and an event that is not understood.	A story that has risk, excitement, or danger

Write the type of fiction that goes with each sentence.

The clues led to the crayon thief. _____

Grandma used to tell me a family story. _____

Betsy lived in Philadelphia in 1767. _____

Sarah went to the beach with Sam. _____

"Excuse me," said the Lion to the boy . _____

Dina and Derek found themselves lost. _____

"We are going out for pizza," said Dad. _____

Fiction

Write the fiction type on the line under the book.

Historical Fiction	Realistic Fiction	Fantasy
Folktales	Mystery	Adventure

Traveling with George Washington

The Case of the Missing Monkey

Dax's Family Trip

_____

The Fish Who Gave Me Advice

Alone in the Woods

Johnny Appleseed

_____

What type of fiction would have the character living in the past?

_____

_____

_____ walks with Jesus.

Writing Drama

Drama is a story (play) that is acted out by others.

Characters	Narrator	Setting
People in the play	Character in the play who tells the audience what is going on	When and where the play takes place

Script - written play which includes:

Dialogue	Stage Directions	Act/Scene
Words the characters speak. Use quotation marks. " "	Directions (where to go, how to move, when to speak) the actors follow	The play is divided into acts and scenes

Script
Act 2
Scene 1

 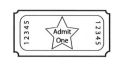

(Curtain opens and, narrator is on the left. Tammy and Brie are sitting on a bench in front of the school.)

Narrator: "It was just four years ago that Tammy met Brie."

Tammy: (Turning to Brie) "I'm so glad we became friends."

Brie: (Eating her ice cream cone) "Me too! We've had so much fun together. Remember when we played hide and seek!"

Tammy: (Laughing) "Yes, we fell in a ditch and looked like mud monsters."

Writing Drama

Look at the script on the last page. Highlight all the stage directions. Then, answer the questions below.

Who are the characters in the drama? _____

_____

What scene is it ? _____

What act is it?_____

What made Tammy Laugh? _____

_____

Draw a line to match the words to the element of drama.

Fred and Wanda   characters

The beginning
of the play.   stage
                                                                     directions

The person who keeps
the audience informed.   setting

At the movie theater   Dialogue

(Walks to the counter
and begins to clean up
the spilled milk)   narrator

                                                                     Act 1
"What surprise do you
have for me, Wanda?"

Week 33   God cares about _____.

Prewriting

Prewriting is thinking!

Purpose	Topic	Brainstorm	Organize
What kind of writing will you be doing? Fiction or Nonfiction	What will you write about?	Write down as many ideas as you can about your topic.	Create a plan to put your writing in order.

Nonfiction Writing

Topic sentence: I went to Pasta House on a field trip.

Five Senses:

I saw: giant loaves of bread	I touched: sticky dough	I tasted: sweet sauce	I heard: waiters calling out orders	I smelled: chefs cooking garlic

Inside Feelings and Thoughts:
I wondered if it was hard to make pasta.
I thought it was hot in the kitchen.

First, I watched the chefs working in the kitchen where it was hot.	**Next,** I lost my family when I stopped to talk to a chef.	**Finally,** I found my family and learned about making a pasta dinner.

Conclusion:
I decided that I was going to be a chef when I grow up.

Prewriting

Fill out this graphic organizer to create a plan for writing.

Topic sentence

_____

_____

Five Senses

I saw:	I touched:	I tasted:	I heard:	I smelled:
_____	_____	_____	_____	_____
_____	_____	_____	_____	_____
_____	_____	_____	_____	_____
_____	_____	_____	_____	_____
_____	_____	_____	_____	_____

Inside feelings and thoughts

_____

_____

First, I _____	Next, I _____	Finally, I _____
_____	_____	_____
_____	_____	_____
_____	_____	_____
_____	_____	_____

Conclusion

_____

_____

_____ trusts in Jesus.

1st Draft

A writer organizes ideas into sentences and paragraphs called a draft. The draft will change as the writer works to make it better.

As you write, check off what you've done:

characters ☑   setting ☑   problem ☑

solution ☑   complete sentences ☑

Pasta House

I enjoy eating pasta! My mom took me and Sandy on a field trip to pasta house. it is my favorite place to eat when we got their, they took us to the kitchen to wash our hands and learn rules. First they took us to watch the cooks One cook was working with dough. He was making bread. We helped kneed the dough. It felt sticky on our hands Then, we watched a cook make spaghetti sauce. She added meat and spices. We each got a to taste it. It was sweet and yummy I stopped to talk to the chef. i told her that I wanted to be just like her. When I looked up, my mom and Sandy were gone. I was scared. All I could hear was noise. The owner came back and found me. We finished the tour with spaghetti!

1st Draft

As you write, check off what you've done:

characters ☐   setting ☐   problem ☐

solution ☐   complete sentences ☐

Use your prewrite to write your 1st draft on the lines below.

_____

_____

_____

_____

_____

_____

_____

_____

_____

_____

_____

_____

_____

God pours His love on _____.

Revise

Writers always reread their writing to make it better. They add words, change words and move things around to sound better.

Add details to your story. ☑ Change words to sound better. ☑
Remove words and sentences that don't make sense. ☑
Move words that would be better somewhere else. ☑
Use a ∧ to add words and ── to take away words. ☑

Pasta House Surprise
For my birthday,   m   ∧   my friend
I enjoy eating pasta! My mom took me and∧sandy on a field trip

to pasta house. it is my favorite place to eat when we got their,

safety
they took us to the kitchen to wash our hands and learn∧rules.

chefs   chef
First they took us to watch the cooks One cook was working with

tasty
dough. He was making∧bread. We helped kneed the dough. It

chef
felt sticky on our hands Then, we watched a cook make

pork, ground beef,   a small bowl
spaghetti sauce. She added meat and spices. We each got∧to

delicious
taste it. It was sweet and yummy. I stopped to talk to the chef.

i told her that I wanted to be just like her. When I looked up, my

worried
mom and Sandy were gone. I was scared. All I could hear was
  of the waiters and chefs as they worked
the noise.∧The owner came back and found me. We finished the
                              and a birthday cake for me
tour with a big plate of spaghetti!∧

2nd Draft: Revise

Use the revise checklist to make your writing better. Fix the mistakes on your 1st draft from yesterday and rewrite it below.

Add details to your story. ☐ Change words to sound better. ☐
Remove words and sentences that don't make sense. ☐
Move words that would be better somewhere else. ☐
Use a ∧ to add words and ‾ to take away words. ☐

Write your 2nd draft on the lines below.

_____

_____

_____

_____

_____

_____

_____

_____

_____

_____

_____

_____

_____

_____

_____ is growing in the Lord.

Edit

Writers always go back and check for mistakes in spelling, capitalization, spacing and punctuation.

Did you start each sentence with a capital letter?   yes   no
Did you end each sentence with punctuation (! . ?)?   yes   no
Did you circle words that you don't know how to spell?   yes   no
Did you write complete sentences?   yes   no
Did you put spaces between words and sentences?   yes   no

Pasta House Surprise

For my birthday, my mom took me and my friend ~~s~~andy on a
field trip to ~~p~~asta ~~h~~ouse. ~~i~~t is my favorite place to eat. ~~w~~hen we
got ~~their~~ (there) they took us to the kitchen to wash or hands and learn

safety rules. First, they took us to watch the chefs. One chef was

working with dough. He was making tasty bread. We helped
~~kneed~~ (knead) the dough. It felt sticky on our hands. Then, we watched

a chef make spaghetti sauce. She added pork, ground beef,

and spices. We each got a small bowel to taste it. It was sweet

and delicious! I stopped to talk to the chef. ~~i~~ told her that I

wanted to be just like her. When I looked up, my mom and

Sandy were gone. I was worried. All I could hear was the noise

of the waiters and chefs as they worked. The owner came back

and found me. We finished the tour with a big plate of spaghetti

and a birthday cake for me!

3rd Draft: Edit

Use the editing checklist to make your writing better. Fix the mistakes on your 2nd draft from yesterday and rewrite it below.

Did you start each sentence with a capital letter?   yes   no
Did you end each sentence with punctuation (! . ?)?   yes   no
Did you circle words that you don't know how to spell?   yes   no
Did you write complete sentences?   yes   no
Did you put spaces between words and sentences?   yes   no

Write your 3rd draft on the lines below.

_____

_____

_____

_____

_____

_____

_____

_____

_____

_____

_____

_____

Publish

Are you ready to publish?

Did you rewrite your story using your best handwriting?	yes	no
Did you make all the changes from your revising?	yes	no
Did you make all the changes from your editing?	yes	no
Did you illustrate your story neatly?	yes	no
Are you ready to share your story with an audience?	yes	no

Pasta House Surprise

For my birthday, my mom took me and my friend Sandy on a field trip to Pasta House. It is my favorite place to eat. When we got there, they took us to the kitchen to wash our hands and learn safety rules. First, they took us to watch the chefs. One chef was working with dough. He was making tasty bread. We helped knead the dough. It felt sticky on our hands. Then, we watched a chef make spaghetti sauce. She added pork, ground beef, and spices. We each got a small bowl to taste it. It was sweet and delicious! I stopped to talk to the chef. I told her that I wanted to be just like her. When I looked up, my mom and Sandy were gone. I was worried. All I could hear was the noise of the waiters and chefs as they worked. The owner came back and found me. We finished the tour with a big plate of spaghetti and a birthday cake for me!

You can publish your work in many ways!

Read it aloud	Make it into a book	Write it on lined paper

Publish

Publish your work by writing it neatly on the lines below and drawing a picture (illustration) to go with it.

Write your new draft on the lines below.

_____

_____

_____

_____

_____

_____

_____

_____

_____

_____

_____

_____

Illustration

A Persuasive Writing: Prewriting

Brainstorm: Write down as many ideas as you can in 5 minutes.

What do you want to persuade people to do?

- learn to play an instrument - eat my favorite meal everyday
- go to an amusement park   - get a pet   - have my own room
- go to the park with friends   - get a new bike   - more free time
- have an allowance   - lunch should always have a dessert

Choose one idea and write a topic sentence.

What do you want to persuade people to do?

Everyone would agree that dessert should always be served with lunch.

Point 1:

Desserts make your meals fun.

Point 2:

Desserts can be healthy.

Reason 1:

Milkshakes are a dessert that is a drink. It is a fun way to have dessert while you eat.

Reason 2:

Fruit cut up in shapes with whipped cream makes a boring meal fun.

Reason 1:

Chocolate pudding has milk. Milk makes you strong.

Reason 2:

Some cakes have fruit. Fruit is a healthy dessert choice.

What do you want to persuade people to do?

Everyone would agree that dessert should always be served with lunch.

Persuasive Writing: Prewriting

Brainstorm: Write down as many ideas as you can in 5 minutes.

What do you want to persuade people to do?

Fill out this graphic organizer.

What do you want to persuade people to do?

_____

_____

Point 1:

_____

_____

Point 2:

_____

_____

Reason 1:

_____

_____

Reason 2:

_____

_____

Reason 1:

_____

_____

Reason 2:

_____

_____

What do you want to persuade people to do?

_____

_____

_____ knows God is faithful.

1st Draft

A good writer uses a plan to create a 1st draft.
Focus on writing complete sentences about your topic.

As you write, check off what you've done:

persuasive topic sentence ☑ conclusion sentence ☑

point 1 ☑   reason 1 ☑   reason 2 ☑

point 2 ☑   reason 1 ☑   reason 2 ☑

Use your prewriting to write
your 1st draft

Lunch and Desert

Everyone knows that lunch should always come with desert.

First it makes meals fun. milkshakes are are a desert that is a drink.

I like to drink milkshakes. It is a fun way with lunch Fruit in shapes

with whipped cream is tasty and the shapes are fun. Second

deserts can be healthy. Chocolate pudding has milk in it. fruit is a

healthy desert. Milk makes you strong. Fruit has a lot of good vita-

mins Everyone would agree that lunch should always coem with

desert.

Persuasive Writing: 1st Draft

As you write, check off what you've done:

persuasive topic sentence ☐   conclusion sentence ☐

point 1 ☐   reason 1 ☐   reason 2 ☐

point 2 ☐   reason 1 ☐   reason 2 ☐

Use your prewriting to write your 1st draft below.

_____

_____

_____

_____

_____

_____

_____

_____

_____

_____

_____

_____

_____

_____

Revising a Persuasive Writing

A good writer rereads what has been written and makes changes to it. There are many ways to make changes: add details, change words, remove words that don't sound good, and move words to a different part of the writing.

Add details to your writing. ☑ Change words to sound better. ☑
Remove words and sentences that don't make sense. ☑
Move words that would be better somewhere else. ☑
Use a ∧ to add words and —— to take away words. ☑

Lunch and Desert

would agree
Everyone ~~knows~~ that lunch should always come with desert.
       ∧
              A   is
First it makes meals fun. milkshakes ~~are are~~ a desert that is a drink.
           ∧   to have desert while you eat
~~Hike to drink milkshakes.~~ It is a fun way ~~with~~ lunch Fruit ~~in~~ shapes
                 are   ∧
with whipped cream ~~is~~ tasty and the shapes are fun. Second
                      is made with
deserts can be healthy. Chocolate pudding ~~has~~ milk in it. ~~fruit is~~
               Pies have fruit in them. ∧
~~a healthy desert.~~ Milk makes you strong. Fruit has a lot of good
     fruit is a healthy desert   ∧
vitamins Everyone would agree that lunch should always coem
     ∧

with desert.

2nd Draft: Revise

Use the revise checklist to make your 1st draft better.

Add details to your essay. ☑ Change words to sound better. ☑
Remove words and sentences that don't make sense. ☑
Move words that would be better somewhere else. ☑
Use a ∧ to add words and —— to take away words. ☑

Write your 2nd draft on the lines below.

_____

_____

_____

_____

_____

_____

_____

_____

_____

_____

_____

_____

_____

Editing a Persuasive Writing

A good writer always goes back and checks for mistakes in spelling, capitalization, spacing, and punctuation.

Did you start each sentence with a capital letter?   yes   no

Did you end each sentence with punctuation (! . ?)?   yes   no

Did you circle words that you don't know how to spell?   yes   no

Did you write complete sentences?   yes   no

Did you put spaces between words and sentences?   yes   no

 Lunch and (Desert)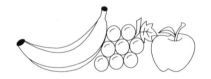

Everyone would agree that lunch should always come with

(desert). First, it makes meals fun. A milkshake is a (desert) that is a

drink. They are a fun way to have (desert) while you eat

lunch. Fruit shapes with whipped cream are tasty and the

shapes are fun. Second, (deserts) can be healthy. Chocolate

pudding is made with milk in it. Milk makes you strong. Pies have

fruit in them. Fruit has a lot of good vitamins. F fruit is a healthy

(desert). Everyone would agree that lunch should always (coem)

with (desert)

3rd Draft: Edit

Use the editing checklist to make your 2nd draft better. Fix the mistakes on your 2nd draft from yesterday and rewrite it below.

Did you start each sentence with a capital letter?   yes no

Did you end each sentence with punctuation (! . ?)?   yes no

Did you circle words that you don't know how to spell? yes no

Did you write complete sentences?   yes no

Did you put spaces between words and sentences? yes no

Write your 3rd draft on the lines below.

_____

_____

_____

_____

_____

_____

_____

_____

_____

_____

_____

_____

Publishing a Persuasive Writing

Writers publish their best work!

Are you ready to publish?

Did you rewrite your story using your best handwriting?   yes   no

Did you make all the changes from your revising?   yes   no

Did you make all the changes from your editing?   yes   no

Are you ready to share your writing with an audience? yes   no

Lunch and Dessert

Everyone would agree that lunch should always come with dessert. First, it makes meals fun. A milkshake is a dessert that is a drink. It is a fun way to have dessert while you eat lunch. Fruit shapes with whipped cream are tasty and the shapes are fun. Second, desserts can be healthy. Chocolate pudding has milk in it. Milk makes you strong. Pies have fruit in them. Fruit has a lot of good vitamins. Fruit is a healthy dessert. Everyone would agree that lunch should always come with dessert.

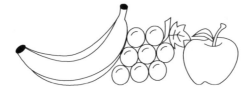

Publishing a Persuasive Writing

Publish your work by writing it neatly on the lines below.

_____

_____

_____

_____

_____

_____

_____

_____

_____

_____

_____

_____

_____

Circle the way you choose to share your work with others.

Read it aloud

Make it into a book

Write it on lined paper

God is with _____.

An Informative Writing: Prewriting

What subjects do you know a lot about?

stuffed animals	frogs	bears
soccer	bike riding	fire safety
playground rules	swimming	rainbows
fall leaves	Florida	dolphins

Choose one topic you want to tell your audience about.

Topic: Dolphins

Topic Sentence: I can teach you all about dolphins.

Fact 1: Dolphins are mammals not fish.	**Fact 2:** Dolphins can't breathe underwater.	**Fact 3:** Dolphins live together in families. These are called pods.

Conclusion Sentence:

As you can see, I know a lot about dolphins.

Informative Writing: Prewriting

Brainstorm: Write down as many ideas as you can in 5 minutes.

What subjects do you know a lot about?

Fill out this graphic organizer.

Topic: _____

_____

Topic Sentence: _____

_____

Fact 1:	Fact 2:	Fact 3:
_____	_____	_____
_____	_____	_____
_____	_____	_____
_____	_____	_____
_____	_____	_____
_____	_____	_____
_____	_____	_____

Conclusion Sentence: _____

_____

_____

_____ is God's creation.

1st Draft

A good writer uses a plan to create a draft. Focus on writing complete sentences about your topic.

As you write, check off what you've done:

informative topic sentence ☐   conclusion sentence ☐

fact 1 ☐   fact 2 ☐   fact 3 ☐

All About Dolphins

I can teached you all about dolphins. Dolphins our mammals they has hair when born. They are so fun to watch. They fed their babies milk. Dolphins can't breath underwater. The familys are called pods they have lungs. They have to come up to the top of the water to breath. I love to play with dolphins. Dolphins lives together in familys. As you can see, I know a lot about dolphins.

Informative Writing: 1st Draft

As you write, check off what you've done:

informative topic sentence ☐   conclusion sentence ☐

fact 1 ☐   fact 2 ☐   fact 3 ☐

Use your prewriting to write your 1st draft below.

_____

_____

_____

_____

_____

_____

_____

_____

_____

_____

_____

_____

_____

_____

Revising an Informative Writing

A good writer rereads what has been written and makes changes to it. There are many ways to make changes: add details, change words, remove words that don't sound good, and move words to a different part of the writing.

Add details to your essay. ☑ Change words to sound better. ☑

Remove words and sentences that don't make sense. ☑

Move words that would be better somewhere else. ☑

Use a ∧ to add words and —— to take away words. ☑

All About Dolphins

I can teach~~ed~~ you all about dolphins. Dolphins ~~our~~ ^{are}∧

mammals they ~~has~~ ^{have}∧ hair when born. ~~They are so fun to~~

~~watch.~~ They fed their babies milk. Dolphins can't breath

underwater. ~~The familys are called pods~~ they have lungs.

They have to come up to the top of the water to breath. ~~I~~

~~love to play with dolphins.~~ Dolphins lives together in

∧ The familys are called pods

familys. As you can see, I know a lot about dolphins.

2nd Draft: Revise

Use the revise checklist to make your 1st draft better.

Add details to your essay. ☐ Change words to sound better. ☐

Remove words and sentences that don't make sense. ☐

Move words that would be better somewhere else. ☐

Use a Λ to add words and — to take away words. ☐

Write your 2nd draft on the lines below.

_____

_____

_____

_____

_____

_____

_____

_____

_____

_____

_____

_____

_____

_____

_____ is created for good works.

Editing an Informative Writing

A good writer always goes back and checks for mistakes in spelling, capitalization, spacing, and punctuation.

Did you start each sentence with a capital letter?   yes   no

Did you end each sentence with punctuation (! . ?)?   yes   no

Did you circle words that you don't know how to spell?   yes   no

Did you write complete sentences?   yes   no

Did you put spaces between words and sentences?   yes   no

All About Dolphins

I can teach you all about dolphins. Dolphins are

mammals. they have hair when born. They fed their

babies milk. Dolphins can't breath underwater. they have

lungs. They have to come up to the top of the water to

breath Dolphins lives together in familys. The familys are

called pods. As you can see, I know a lot about dolphins.

3rd Draft: Edit

Use the editing checklist to make your writing better. Fix the mistakes on your 2nd draft from yesterday and rewrite it below.

Did you start each sentence with a capital letter?   yes   no
Did you end each sentence with punctuation (! . ?)?   yes   no
Did you circle words that you don't know how to spell?   yes   no
Did you write complete sentences?   yes   no
Did you put spaces between words and sentences?   yes   no

Write your 3rd draft on the lines below.

_____

_____

_____

_____

_____

_____

_____

_____

_____

_____

_____

_____ has faith to believe God.

Publishing an Informative Writing

Writers publish their best work!

Are you ready to publish?
Did you rewrite your story using your best handwriting?   yes   no
Did you make all the changes from your revising?   yes   no
Did you make all the changes from your editing?   yes   no
Did you illustrate your story neatly?   yes   no
Are you ready to share your writing with an audience? yes   no

All About Dolphins

I can teach you all about dolphins. Dolphins are mammals. They

have hair when born. They feed their babies milk. Dolphins can't

breathe underwater. They have lungs. They have to come up to

the top of the water to breathe. Dolphins live together in families.

The families are called pods. As you can see, I know a lot about

dolphins.

Publishing an Informative Writing

Publish your work by writing it neatly on the lines below.

_____

_____

_____

_____

_____

_____

_____

_____

_____

_____

_____

_____

Draw a picture to go with your writing.

Sensory Poems

Sensory Poems use all five senses to describe a feeling or thing.

Sensory poems use similes to show how things are alike.
A simile uses the words **like** or **as**.

Choose a subject (thing or feeling) that you will describe.

What **color** best describes your subject?

If it had a **taste**, what would your subject taste like?

What does your subject **sound** like?

What does your subject **smell** like?

What does your subject **look** like?

How does your subject make you **feel**?

Winter

Winter is Silver

It **tastes** like hot soup on a cold day.

It **sounds** like wind blowing through the trees.

It **smells** like hot chocolate and sweet marshmallows.

It **looks** like coats, scarves, and warm gloves.

It **feels** like love when family gets together for the holidays.

Sensory poems start with choosing one subject
that you want to write about.

What is one subject that you can see, hear, feel, taste and touch?

_____

Writing Sensory Poems

Finish the poem that has been started by filling in the blanks.

The Farm

The farm is red.

It **tastes** like fresh eggs from the chicken coup.

It **sounds** like _____

_____

It **smells** like fresh cut hay to feed the cows.

It **looks** like _____

_____

It **feels** like joy when new animals are born.

Fill out this organizer to write a sensory poem.
Start by writing the subject on the first line.

_____

_____ is _____

It tastes like _____

_____

It sounds like _____

_____

It smells like _____

_____

It looks like _____

_____

It feels like _____

_____

The joy of the Lord is in _____.

Color Poems

Color Poems use **all five senses** to tell about **one color.**

Choose a color that you will describe.

Write a word that goes with the color.

 Write what the color **tastes** like.

Write what the color smells like.

 Write what the color **sounds** like.

Write what the color **feels** like.

Write what the color **looks** like.

Write one thing the color makes you do or **feel.**

Write a word that goes with the color.

Yellow

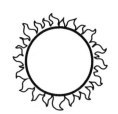
Yellow is sunshine.

Yellow **tastes** like fresh squash.

Yellow **smells** like lemon pie.

Yellow **sounds** like the crackle of a fire.

Yellow **feels** like light on my face.

Yellow **looks** like leaves falling from trees.

Yellow **makes** me think about flowers.

Yellow is happy.

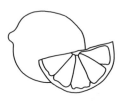

Color poems start with choosing one color that you want to write about. It can be any color. What color would you choose?

_____

Writing Color Poems

Finish the poem that has been started by filling in the blanks.

Brown

Brown is the leaves at the end of fall.

Brown **tastes** like gravy on my turkey.

_____ **smells** like _____

Brown **sounds** like acorns falling from a tree.

_____ **feels** like _____

_____ **looks** like _____

Brown **makes** me think about chocolate kisses.

_____ **is** _____

Fill out this organizer to write your own color poem.

_____

_____ **is** _____

_____ tastes like _____

_____ smells like _____

_____ sounds like _____

_____ feels like _____

_____ looks like _____

_____ makes me _____

_____ **is** _____

Jesus is Lord of _____.

Cinquain Poems

Cinquain poems have five lines. Each line uses a part of speech.

Write one **noun** (person, place, or thing).

Write two **adjectives**.

Write three **verbs** that end in -ing.

Write a four word phrase that describes the **noun**.

Write a word that is another name for the **noun**.

Here are a few thing we know about the noun ocean.

There is sand.   Crabs crawl on the sand.

The water moves.   Sunshine makes it hot.

People swim in the ocean.   Lifeguards keep everyone safe.

Kids make sand castles.   Fishing and collecting shells.

ocean
noun

wavy
adjective

playful
adjective

dancing
verb with -ing

swimming
verb with -ing

changing
verb with -ing

kids make sand castles
four word phrase that describes the noun

beach
noun

Writing Cinquain Poems

Write everything you know about the noun bluebird.

Finish the poem that has been started by filling in the blanks.

bluebird
noun

_____ musical
adjective   adjective

_____ nesting _____
verb with -ing verb with -ing verb with -ing

looking for juicy worms
four word phrase that describes the noun

songbird
noun

Choose a noun and write everything you know about the noun.

_____
noun

_____ _____
adjective   adjective

_____ _____ _____
verb with -ing verb with -ing verb with -ing

_____ _____ _____ _____
four word phrase that describes the noun

_____
noun

Haiku Poems

Haiku poems have three lines. Each line has a different syllable.

Choose a word to write about.

Write a line that describes your word and has five syllables.
Write a line that describes your word and has seven syllables.
Write a line that describes your word and has five syllables.

Puppies
What is the poem about?

Little balls of fur
Describe your word with **five syllables**.

Jumping all around the house
Describe your word with **seven syllables**.

They are just so cute
Describe your word with **five syllables**.

Finish the last line of this haiku poem.

Rainbows
What is the poem about?

They hang in the sky.
Describe your word with **five syllables**.

Rainbows are so colorful.
Describe your word with **seven syllables**.

_____

Describe your word with **five syllables**.

Writing Haiku Poems

Read the haiku poem and write the word the haiku is describing.

_____
What is the poem about?

They crawl on eight legs.
They trap insects on their webs.
I do not like them!
Arachnid

Write two haiku poems.

_____
What is the poem about?

_____
Describe your word with **five syllables.**

_____
Describe your word with **seven syllables**

_____
Describe your word with **five syllables.**

_____
What is the poem about?

_____
Describe your word with **five syllables.**

_____
Describe your word with **seven syllables**

_____
Describe your word with **five syllables.**

God gives grace to _____.

Writing an Acrostic Poem

Acrostic poems use the first letter of each
word to spells out a word vertically.

Choose a word to write about.

Write the word vertically.

Write a line for each letter of the word.

Learning to build

Enjoying the time

Great for rainy days

Organize the pieces

Giving is better than receiving.

I love to make others smile

Freely given

Thank you

Write your own acrostic poem and draw a picture to go with it.

Writing a Shape Poem

A shape poem chooses a word to write about.
The poem is then written in the shape of that word.

Choose a word to write about.
Write words that describe the shape.
Rewrite the words in the shape of the poem.

I gave Him my heart
because He gave His life.
Jesus gave His all for me.
He loved me before, He will
always love me.

Write your poem on the lines
first. Then write it in a shape.

_____

_____

_____

_____

_____

_____

_____

Answer Keys

Unit 4 Week 19 Answer Key

Prefix, Suffix, and Base Words

in**complete**	**heal**thy	pre**vent**
re**store**	sub**way**	in**expensive**
re**use**	**pray**ed	**talk**ing
stronger	**clean**est	**safe**ly
restful	**effort**less	un**pack**

Affixes and Base Words

reheat	thankful
preheat	thankless
recook	cheerful
precook	cheerless
unfair	mixer

Prefixes

un — read — reread
re — pay — prepay
in — true — untrue
pre — title — subtitle
re — valid — invalid
sub — act — react

More Prefixes

de	decrease
im	immature
de	deflate
im	impatient
de	decode
dis	disagree
dis	disconnect

Prefixes

midnight
nonfat
misjudge
nonfiction
misfiled
midstream
nonsense

Vowel Suffixes

taller	tallest	act of swinging
		able to respond
longer	longest	more than one fox
		paint in the past
shorter	shortest	able to wash
		condition of having a
smaller	smallest	lot of wing

Consonant Suffixes

ly	ful
less	ness
ness	less
ment	ly
ion	ment
ful	ion

Vowel and Consonant Suffixes

lengthwise
elevator
actor
mountainous
dangerous
clockwise
courageous

Prefix and Suffix Review

inspector	**weak**ness	**midweek**
unsafe	**cross**wise	**power**ful
retry	**danc**ed	**quick**ly
suitable	**cold**er	**de**fog
subside	**in**visible	**place**ment
permissible	**rich**est	**home**less
impolite	**throw**ing	**adventur**ous
latches	**mess**y	**non**dairy
misspell	**pre**view	**dis**like
		decoration

Crossword Review

```
            LIKEWISE      B
                GRACEFUL
D      DISTRUST        M
A        SOFTNESS      P
R          RASHES      Y    C   V    F
K      NONFAT               O   I    I
E      USELESS              L   S    L
R        UNWISE             D   I    L
  REPLAY                    L   T    I
  LIKED                     Y   O    N
                               R    G
```

Unit 4 Week 20 Answer Key

Prefixes and Suffixes

able	able to wash	ible	able to have sense
es	more than one church	able	able to break
ible	not able to believe	es	more than one dish
able	able to profit	es	more than one potato
es	more than one glass	ible	able to respond

Suffixes

agreement	government
baldness	likeness
blindness	subtraction
reflection	measurement

Suffix Rule: Double the Consonant

clapped	clapping
trimmed	trimming
spotted	spotting
crammed	cramming
chopped	chopping

Suffix Rule: Keep the y

red	green	red
green	red	green
green	green	red

Suffix Rule: Change the y to an i

plentiful	tried
armies	riskier
joyful	beautiful
crying	

Suffix Rule: Change ie to y

lying - sentence will vary

tying - sentence will vary

dying - sentence will vary

Suffix Rule: Drop the Silent e

driving	riding
taking	baking
making	writing
hiding	

Suffix Rule: Keep the Silent e

balancing	closely
piecing	freely
eyeing	charging

Suffix Review

families	slimming	busier	goodness
likeable	hottest	lovely	reflection
awareness	closely	inspiration	bunnies
responsible	shipment	easier	libraries

JESUS LOVES YOU

fulfill — ing
shop — er
stay — ment
wake — ed
glance — ing
fry — er

Unit 4 Week 21 Answer Key

Homonyms

(there/their)   can/can   wind/wind

park/park   (cent/sent)

(who's/whose)   (night/knight)   (by/buy)

(there/they're)   (scent/sent)

palm/palm   fly/fly

duck/duck   (bye/buy)   (your/you're)

Homophones

their
They're
their
They're
their
there
they're

Homophones

who's
✓
✓
your
✓
✓
who's

More Homophones

scent
boy
sent
by
cent
bye
by

Homographs

fly   duck
fly   duck
bat
bat   sentences will vary

More Homographs

palm   can
palm   can
park
park   sentences will vary

Homographs

minute
agape
moped
moped
agape
minute

More Homographs

buffet
wind
buffet
tear
wind
tear

Homonym Review

cent   scent
there   their
who's   whose
buy   by
they're   their
your   you're

_____ going to get a family picture   I saw my dog wave _____   I needed one _____ to buy an apple.

agape   they're   duck   cent   bye   who's

I told my friend to _____ so he didn't get hit.   _____ going to watch the game?   God's love for us is _____ love.

sentences will vary

Unit 4 Week 22 Answer Key

Syllables

m**a**p

tr**u**ck

sn**a**p

h**u**m

Counting Syllables

basket	2	mug	1
flower	2	cookie	2
test	1	kazoo	2
lemon	2	cube	1
bench	1	airplane	2

Open Syllables

e / ven	pi / lot	o / pen	de / frost
hel / lo	stu / dent	mu / sic	a / pron
bo / nus	be / yond	car / go	be / gin
lo / cate	mo / ment	ho / tel	u / nit
re / cite	po / lo	pro / tect	

Closed Syllables

o / ver	hu / man	pro / tect	ra / zor
ro / dent	vi / tal	hap / pen	ba / sis
fro / zen	cra / tor	fe / ver	zer / o
si / ren	ham / mer	jo / ker	cat / nap
in / flate	hel / met	med / ding	

Vowel + Consonant + e Syllables

ex / plode	ad / vice	sun / rise
com / pare	in / side	in / side
cup / cake	con / fuse	ex / plode
sun / rise		con / fuse

ad / vice   cup / cake   com / pare

Long o Words

see	1	flounder	2
enjoy	2	window	2
await	2	day	1
outbreak	2	needle	2
weapon	2	flea	1

R-Controlled Syllables

barber	church
artwork	tiger
certain	flavor
comfort	acorns

Consonant + le Syllables

jungle	struggle
freckles	waddle
people	grumble
nibble	

sentences and word choice will vary

Multi-Syllabic Words

notebook	2	queen	1	donut	2	detective	3
skew	1	thanksgiving	3	elephant	3	once	1
octopus	3	softly	2	mask	1	bunny	2
butterfly	3	jellyfish	3	taco	2	strawberry	3
evergreen	3	clam	1	almost	2	broccoli	3

dandelion - 4

Multi-Syllabic Words

closed	closed		open	open	closed
closed	open		open	open	closed
open	closed		closed	open	closed
closed	closed		open	open	closed
open	closed		open	open	closed
			closed	open	closed
			open	open	open

Unit 4 Week 23 Answer Key

Syllables Rule #1

g(ar)den   gar / den   p(ar)ty   par / ty

f(or)get   for / get   pl(ur)al   plur / al

(ar)gue   ar / gue   b(ur)ger   bur / ger

t(ar)get   tar / get   (ur)chin   ur / chin

w(or)ship   wor / ship   b(ar)gain   bar / gain

Syllable Rule #2

vel / vet   ex / am   gav / el   mag / net

o / dor   sand / wich   ti / ger   cab / in

laugh / ter   doc / tor   un / til   Word choice and sentence will vary.

ex / cite   bas / ket   ze / bra

fin / ish   be / low   rob / in

Syllables Rule #3

pup/ py   jig / gle   lit / tle

scis / sors   ham / mer   din / ner

fun / ny   spar / row   puz / zle

com / ma   mil / lion   Word choice and sentences will vary.

mess / y   let / tuce

Syllables Rule #4

fal / con   chap / ter

wis / dom   ab / sent

nap / kin   plas / tic

in / sect

sub / ject

Syllables Rule #5

o / pen   giv / en   rob / in   pi / lot

va / cant   fin / ish   su / per   Fri / day

tal / ent   ba / by   com / ic   vis / it

ti / ger   sev / en   le / mon   mu / sic

Syllables Rule #6

rain / bow   pan / cake

jelly / fish   cup / cake

snow / man   sun / flower

butter / fly   cow / boy

    tooth / brush

Syllables Rule #7

ost	rich	ostrich
ther	mos	thermos
sun	shine	sunshine
whis	per	whisper
re	main	remain
pay	ee	payee
pur	sue	pursue
up	load	upload
ea	ger	eager

Syllables Rule #8

jolt	ed	jolted
grump	y	grumpy
laun	dry	laundry
skip	per	skipper
spi	nal	spinal
her	ald	herald
clus	ter	cluster
pret	zel	pretzel
skip	per	skipper
threat	en	threaten
my	self	myself

Syllables Rule #9

re / read   in / tend   im / pose   re / do

in / vent   un / paid   un / wrap   im / press

pre / fer   re / buy   pre / dict   un / safe

im / age   in / sist   re / turn

un / well   pre / cise   word choice and sentences will vary.

Syllables Rule #10

hum / ble   waf / fle

can / dle   ma / ple

driz / zle   bea /gle

cir / cle   bat / tle

Unit 4 Week 24 Answer Key

Prefix Review

mid	midpoint
pre	predict
sub	submarine
non	nonstick
im	imperfect
de	deactivate
re	repaint
mis	misjudge
un	unaware
in	inactive
dis	disappear

Suffix Review

ible	incredible	The family was
ed	excited	brave when they
ous	beautiful	touched the
ful	movement	stingrays.
ment	enjoyable	
able	closer	
er	coldest	
est	smelly	
ly	hanging	
ing	courageous	
ness		

Suffix Spelling Review

hammer	clipped
dropping	planner
sliceable	courageous
peaceable	outrageous
parties	bodily
vying	dying
timing	ruling
muting	bitting
flying	drying
applying	supplying

Is it Spelled Right?

dimmer	shyness
stories	dryly
shaking	swimming
daily	taking
tying	juiceable
forceable	

Homophones

buy	bye
You're	They're
their	Your
sent	cent
Who's	by
scent	There
Whose	

Homographs

b. travel in the sky   laid around feeling sad

a. an animal

a. air blowing   a part of the hand

b. place to visit

b. a container

Syllable Review

1	2	3	4
none	lady	wonderful	watermelon
wise	jigsaw	pajama	helicopter
tree	sandwich	cucumber	television
purse	donate	fantastic	alligator

Syllable Review

um/brel/la	closed	fin/ger/print	closed
bi/cy/cle	open	ta/ken	open
po/ny/tail	open	lem/on/ade	closed
to/ma/to	open	blue/ber/ry	closed
bo/nus	open	grass/hop/er	closed
ex/cit/ed	closed	jan/u/ary	closed

o/pin/ion
mim/ic
for/get/ful

Syllable Division Review

ex/it	2,5	fab/ric	2,4	be/gin	2,5
tick/lish	2,4,5,7	sham/poo	2,4,7	es/teem	2,4,7
un/cle	2,4,5,10	wild/life	2,4,6	itch/y	2,7
mis/sion	2,3,7	sub/tract	2,4,8	mar/ket	1,2,4
char/coal	1,2,4,7	fum/ble	2,4,5,10	com/et	2,5
hand/stand	2,4,6	fros/ting	2,8	num/ber	1245
mop/ping	2,3,5	tu/lip	2,5	in/form	1245
		tea/cup	2,6,7	pil/low	2,4,5

Dividing Syllables Review

po/ny/tail	whis/per	word choice and sentences will vary
writ/ten	pump/kin	
ice/pack	slip/per	
ex/plain	frigh/ten	
mis/match	gar/den	
fla/vor		

Unit 5 Week 25 Answer Key

Punctuation Marks

Sammy shouted, "Jesus loves me __!__ "

On Sundays I go to church to worship Jesus __.__

Why do tigers have stripes on them __?__

Stop the car __!__

Jesus is the Son of God __.__

End Marks

		Sentences:
C	!	
?	C	Answers will
!	?	vary.
C	!	
C	?	

Apostrophes

singular
plural
singular
plural
plural
plural

Possessive Nouns

Emma's
deer's
Mrs. Peters'
scissor's
cow's
Chris'
chefs'
Mary's

Contractions

can't
should've
he's
won't
I'm

More Contractions

I	am	they're	can't
she	is	he's	would've
should	have	didn't	you're
are	not	we're	isn't
could	have	it's	I've
will	not		

Commas

Manuel lived in Seattle, Washington for six years.

Some scholars record the first resurrection on April 23, 33 AD.

The zoo opened in Norfolk, Virginia on March 5, 1900.

More Commas

shirt,
Los Angeles,
flour, oranges,
First,
Next,
steak, zucchini, salad,
Jesus,

Punctuation Letter Review

Jorge,		hotdogs, hamburgers,
I'm	news!	pizza, spaghetti.
It's	Tonya's	don't
you.	come?	
house.Memphis,		swim?
games,		June 5, Sincerely,
There's	We're	.

Punctuation Review

bees' honey
pastor's Bible
children's toys
mice's cheese
Lord's favor
ocean's waves

.
?

Unit 5 Week 26 Answer Key

Abbreviating Titles

Mrs. Harriet

John Wilson, Sr.

Mr. George Eicker

Calvin Jr.

More Titles

Mrs. Wilson	Gen. George Washington
Prof. Blackstone	Pres. John Adams
Dr. Phillips	Capt. Karl Branchy
Pr. Frank Farrell	Mr. Tommy Smiggles
Paul Quail, Sr.	Gov. William Franklin

Abbreviating Days of the week

Tues.	Sentences:
Sat.	
Mon.	
Thurs.	Answers will
Sun.	vary.
Wed.	
Fri.	

Days of the week

Wednesday	Wed.
Monday	Mon.
Thursday	Thurs.
Tuesday	Tues.
Saturday	Sat.
Friday	Fri.

Abbreviating Months

Feb.	Jun.	May
Jan.	Mar.	Apr.

More Months

Oct.   Sept.   Jul.

Dec.   Nov.   Aug.

July — Aug.
August — Dec.
September — Oct.
October — Jul.
November — Sept.
December — Nov.

Abbreviating English Measurements

1/2 c.	1 c.
1 tbsp.	
	2 c.
1 tsp.	1/2 tsp.
12 oz.	

More English Measurements

miles	mi.
yard yards	yd. / yds.
inches	in.
centimeters	cm.
pounds	lbs.
millimeters	mm.
feet meter	ft. / m.
feet	ft.

Abbreviations Review

Mon.	Wed.
Gen.	Dec.
qts.	pt.
Mrs.	oz.
tsp.	Nov.
c.	Sun.

Abbreviations Review

Carl White Junior
Governor Jackson
Professor Robert Oak
Mister Larzon
Pastor Doug Newell
Misses Emily Grason
President Trump
Captain Mike Walls

Prof.
Mrs.
Pres.
Ps.
Capt.
Gov.
Mr.
Jr.

in.

lbs.

mi.

vol.

yd.

Unit 5 Week 27 Answer Key

Nouns and Adjectives

How does it feel?
How does it taste?
What size?
How does it look?
How does it behave?
What shape?
How does it smell?

Adjectives

beautiful	beautiful	Sentences:
five	colorful	
huge	royal	Answers will vary.
burning	wood	
loving		

Articles

a	the
a	the
the	an
a	an
a	

Nouns, Adjectives, and Articles

answers will vary

a	a	a
an	an	a
a	a	an
an	a	an

new movie   blue iPad
best friend   funny joke
little girl   brother   chewy cookie
handsome farmer   tall trees
cute t-shirts   computer

Verbs and Adverbs

Where?
To what extent?
How?
When?
How?

Adverbs

always
Before
now
carefully
every
excitedly
often
gently

Nouns, Adjectives, Verbs and Adverbs

noun
adverb
verb
adjective
adjective
adverb
verb

Nouns and Adjectives

answers will vary

A Silly Day with My Cousin

answers will vary

Verbs and Adverbs

answers will vary

Unit 5 Week 28 Answer Key

Simple Subjects and Predicates

subject	subject
subject	predicate
predicate	predicate
subject	

Subjects and Predicates

(noun)		(verb)	
Callie	Abbie	enjoys	found
Ryan	George	flew	gave
Tim	Izzy	cleans	arrived
Jimena	Barbara	responded	climbs
Carla	Debbie	collects	slipped
Eli	Jose		

Writing Simple Parts of Speech

All answers
will vary

More Simple Parts of Speech

subject	predicate
predicate	subject
predicate	predicate
subject	predicate
subject	subject
subject	predicate

Complete Subjects and Predicates

predicate	predicate
subject	predicate
subject	subject
predicate	subject

Subjects and Predicates

The Lord God	was the son of Jacob and Rachel.
God	loved his son very much.
Noah's	was given to Joseph as a gift.
When the time was right, God	sold him to be a slave in Egypt.
The animals	rested upon Joseph.
The flood	had a dream that only Joseph could interpret.
A rainbow	became a mighty leader in Egypt.

Writing complete Subjects and Predicates

All answers
will vary

Subject and Predicate Review

Percy	All
pastor	sentences
church	will vary
knight	
sister	

Complete Subjects and Predicates

Jonah was a prophet of the Lord.

One day God told Jonah to go to Nineveh.

The people of Nineveh were very evil.

Prophet Jonah did not want to go.

He boarded a ship going in the opposite direction.

A bad storm came against the ship.

The wooden ship started to sink.

All of the workers threw things off the ship.

Disobedient Jonah was asleep in the ship.

The captain woke Jonah up.

The terrible storm would stop when they threw Jonah overboard.

A huge fish swallowed Jonah.

Jonah was in the fish for three days.

The fish spit Jonah out.

The people of Nineveh heard the message and repented.

Subject and Predicate Review

took

fasted   prayed

wrote

took

built

All sentences will vary

Unit 5 Week 29 Answer Key

Diagramming Sentences

predicate line

base line | subject (noun) | predicate (verb)

Robert | swings

Diagramming Simple Sentences

Mr. Snowman | melted   Kevin | gave

Governor Randolph | served   people | clapped

Grace Ann | flew   Allen | played

Diagramming with Adjectives

predicate line

base line | subject | predicate

Article   Adjective

snowflake | melted   lady | cooked
A / pretty   The / sweet

walrus | smiled   man | taught
A / happy   An / educated

cake | tipped   tiger | growled
The / perfect   An / orange

Diagramming with Adverbs

predicate line

base line | subject | predicate

Adverb

Pastor | preached   Miguel | laughed
\ lovingly   \ a lot

Isa | jumps   Lions | hunt
\ always   \ swiftly

Bears | growl   Puppies | bark
\ wildly   \ constantly

Diagramming with Adjectives and Adverbs

predicate line

base line | subject | predicate

Article   Adjective   Adverb

kitten | meowed   snake | crawled
The / fluffy \ softly   The / green \ sneakily

octopus | inks   cat | licks
An / elegant \ often   A / playful \ frequently

leader | spoke   operator | called
The / smart \ afterwards An / eager \ today

People | talk   clown | danced
\ excitedly   The \ crazy

sailboat | sailed   artist | painted
A / blue   The / nice \ beautifully

singer | sings   actors | sobbed
The / pretty \ professionally   \ successfully

Blaire | smiled   captain | joked
                          The / funny

Audiences | applauded   care | raced
\ wildly   A / sporty \ madly

fish | swam   girl | heard
The / colorful \ freely   The / praying \ clearly

Unit 5 Week 30 Answer Key

Punctuation Review

The tree's leave

The painter's paint

The woman's jewelry

The caterpillar's cocoon

God's Word

Birds' wings

Transformation

life.	happening,
friends.	new.
laughing,	days,
talking,	wings.
together,	sun's
gone?	That's
them,	too!
didn't	them.

Abbreviations Review

Mister - Mr.	October - Oct.
Monday - Mon.	Wednesday - Wed.
March - Mar.	Junior - Jr.
yard - yd.	Professor - Prof.
cup - c.	December - Dec.
Misses - Mrs.	inches - in.

More Abbreviations

cm. - centimeter	mm. - millimeter
Sr. - Senior	Gov. - Governor
mi. - mile	Fri. - Friday
Pres. - President	lb. - pound
Apr. - April	tsp. - teaspoon
tbsp. - tablespoon	Jan. - January
Capt. - Captain	Thurs. - Thursday
Sat. - Saturday	pt. - pint

Parts of Speech Review

adverb	adverb
adjective	adjective
adverb	adverb
adjective	adverb
adjective	adverb
adjective	

Adjectives and Adverb Review

rough fisherman	follow obediently
Peaceful Jesus	quickly went
huge crowd	threw once
wooden boat	collect rapidly
eager crowd	hurriedly cried
deep water	completely filled
great catch	left everything
empty nets	

Subjects and Predicates Review

Israelites lived	mother placed
Pharaoh made	basket placed
Israelites cried	daughter watched
people asked	princess found
God sent	She called
Pharaoh decided	woman adopted
woman hid	

More Subjects and Predicates

answers will vary

Jesus	taught
	lovingly

timer	beeped
A	loud

preacher	gave
The	kind / generously

lady	prayed
The	sweet

cat	ran
An	orange / inside

Birds	fly
	often

Diagramming Sentences

Jesus	saves

teacher	taught
A	perfect

children	played
	loudly

musician	played
The	fine / easily

answers will vary

Unit 6 Week 31 Answer Key

Opinion Writing	Opinion Writing All answers will vary
Persuasive Writing	Persuasive Writing All answers will vary
Informative Writing	Informative Writing All answers will vary
Narrative Writing	Narrative Writing All answers will vary
Types of Writing Review Informative Persuasve opinion narrative	More Review opinion narrative Informative persuasive

Unit 6 Week 32 Answer Key

Color and Sensory Poems

answers will vary

A bird

Acrostic and Shape Poems

dolphin   shape

answers will vary   barks, tricks,

answers will vary   and bones

Cinquain and Haiku Poems

three   sea turtles

beach   seven

sandy, salty   laying eggs, following

the moon, or swimming

Rhyming Poems

test and best   answers will vary

done and won   stall

no

Sally prayed for
help on her test.

Types of Nonfiction Writing

diary/journal   letter
informational   autobiography
biography   informational or
essay   article

Nonfiction

Biography   Informational Text   Letter

Autobiography   Essay/Article   Diary/Journal

Autobiography

Types of Fiction Writing

Mystery   Fantasy
Folktales   Adventure
Historical Fiction   Realistic Fiction
Realistic Fiction

Fiction

Historical Fiction   Mystery   Realistic Fiction

Fantasy   Adventure   Folktale

Historical Fiction

Writing Drama

Fred and Wanda — characters
The beginning
of the play.
The person who keeps — stage
the audience informed.
At the movie theater — directions
(Walks to the counter — setting
and begins to clean up
the spilled milk) — Dialogue
"What surprise do you — narrator
have for me, Wanda?" — Act 1

Unit 6 Week 33-36
Answer Key

Answers will vary

Unit 4
Resources

Prefixes

in - not

in + expensive = **in**expensive

meaning: not costly, cheap

 10¢

un - not

un + lock = **un**lock

meaning: open the lock by using a key

---

re - again

re + wind = **re**wind

meaning: back to the beginning

pre - before

pre + dict = **pre**dict

meaning: say what will happen in the future

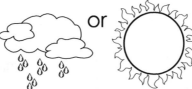

sub - under

sub + tract = **su**tract

meaning: take away from another

```
  6
- 3
  3
```

---

de - opposite of

de + frost = **de**frost

meaning: opposite of freeze

dis - not, opposite

dis + obey = **dis**obey

meaning: opposite of obey

im - not

im + perfect = **im**perfect

meaning: not perfect

---

mid - middle

mid + day = **mid**day

meaning: middle of the day

mis - wrong, bad

mis + deed = **mis**deed

meaning: bad deed

non - without

non + stop = **non**stop

meaning: without stopping

Vowel Suffixes

ed - already happened
laugh + **ed** = laugh**ed**

meaning: to be amused

ing - happening now
jump + **ing** = jump**ing**

meaning: moving in a

specific way

---

er - more than
happy + **er** = happi**er**

meaning: feeling

excited

est - the most
strong + **est** = strong**est**

meaning: power to move

heavy weights

---

able - capable
like + **able** = like**able**

meaning: easy to like

ible - able
flex + **ible** = flex**ible**

meaning: ready and able to

change

---

ous - quality of

zeal + **ous** = zeal**ous**

meaning: quality of having zeal

or - person

direct + **or** = direct**or**

meaning: a person who directs

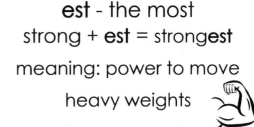

---

ion - action
invent + **ion** = invent**ion**

meaning: action of inventing something

Consonant Suffixes

ful - full of
pain + **ful** = painful

meaning: causing physical pain

less - none
effort + **less** = effortless

meaning: no physical effort

ly - tired
tired + **ly** = tiredly

meaning: the need to rest

ness- state of, condition
kind + **ness** = kindness

meaning: being friendly

wise - relating to

other + **wise** = otherwise

meaning: relating to another way

ment - action
ship + **ment** = shipment

meaning: shipping goods

Suffix Spelling Rules

Double the consonant when:
- a base word has a **short vowel** and **ends with a consonant**.
(Do not double w, x, or y.)

pop ⟶ po**pp**ing

- a base word has more than one syllable, the **second syllable** has a **short vowel** and **ends with a consonant**.

tip ⟶ ti**pp**ing

Keep the **(y)** when:
- a base word ends in a vowel + **(y)**.

play ⟶ playing

- a suffix starting with **(i)** is being added to the base word.

carry ⟶ carrying

Change the **(y)** to an **(i)** when a base word ends in a consonant + **(y)**.

duty ⟶ dutiful

Rule Exception: Keep the **(y)** when the suffix starts with an **(i)**.

dry ⟶ drying

When a word ends in **(ie)**, change **(ie)** to a **(y)** if the suffix starts with **(i)**.

tie ⟶ tying

When a base word ends in a silent (e), drop the (e) and add a **vowel suffix**.

smile ⟶ smiling

Keep the silent (e) when:
- a base word ends in a silent (e) and it is a **consonant suffix**.

active ⟶ actively

- a base word ends in (ee) or (ye).

eye ⟶ eyeing   free ⟶ freeing

- a base word ends in (ce) or (ge) and the suffix starts with an (a) or (o).

notice ⟶ noticeable   outrage ⟶ outrageous

Homonyms - Homophones

Homophones

 Words that sound the same BUT have a different spelling.

there	their (belongs to)	they're (they are)
The ant is **there**.	That is **their** lamb.	**They're** getting married.

your	you're (you are)
That is **your** mitten.	**You're** a singer.

whose	who's (who is)
Whose toy truck is this?	**Who's** that man?

by	buy	bye

She is **by** the desk.	He will **buy** a boat.	They waved **bye**.

cent	scent	sent
Candy is one **cent**.	The **scent** is sweet.	He was **sent** out.

Homonyms - Homophones

Homographs

Words that can sound different
BUT have the same spelling.

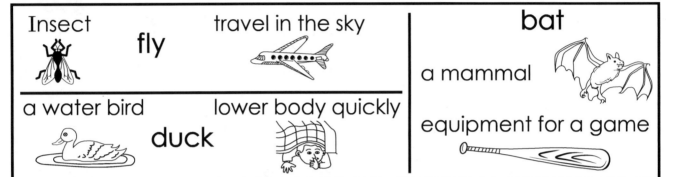

Insect **fly** travel in the sky

a water bird **duck** lower body quickly

bat

a mammal

equipment for a game

can

ability

container

park

put in a space

place to visit

palm

tree

part of hand

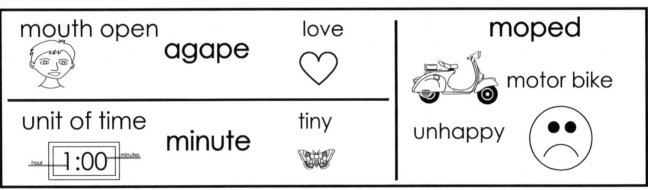

mouth open **agape** love

unit of time **minute** tiny

moped

motor bike

unhappy

wind

air blowing

make a clock work

tear

to cry

rip a paper

buffet

to hit over and over

a meal

Syllables

A syllable is a word part. Every syllable must have one vowel.

You can count syllables by the vowel sounds you hear.

An open syllable has one vowel and does not have a consonant at the end. The vowel sound is long.

<u>me</u>   <u>we</u>   tem/<u>po</u>   <u>pa</u>/per

A closed syllable has a short vowel sound and ends with a consonant.

<u>pig</u>   <u>dog</u>   <u>mon</u>/<u>key</u>

A vowel + consonant + e syllable has a long vowel and a silent e.

b<u>ale</u>   c<u>ape</u>   pan/c<u>ake</u>

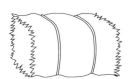   

A vowel team syllable has two vowels next to each other. The vowel team makes only one vowel sound.

tr<u>ai</u>n   t<u>ie</u>   a/sl<u>ee</u>p

An r-controlled syllable has a vowel that is followed by an (r).
The (r) changes the sound of the vowel.

fe/ver　　　　　or/bit　　　　　re/turn

A consonant + le syllable has a consonant followed by (le).
The consonant+ (le) comes at the end of the word.

twin/<u>kle</u>　　　　cat/<u>tle</u>　　　　mar/<u>ble</u>

Many English words have more than one syllable.
We call these multi-syllabic words.
You can count them by listening for the vowel sound.

chick (1)　　　　pret/zel (2)　　　　spa/ghet/ti (3)

Dividing Syllables: Rules 1-5

When dividing syllables, r-controlled vowels (**ar, er, ir, or,** and **ur**) are partners. They always stay together. You divide the syllable after the pair.

 harvest = har / vest

When dividing syllables, all syllables have only **one** vowel sound.

pen/cil   pic/nic   cac/tus

When dividing syllables, divide a two syllable word between twin letters.

cherries = cher/ries   kettle = ket/tle

When dividing syllables, divide the word between two middle consonants when there is a vowel on each side.

dentist = den / tist   marker = mar/ker

When dividing syllables, divide <u>after the consonant</u> when the vowel is **short**.

wag/on

When dividing syllables, divide <u>before the consonant</u> when the vowel is **long**.

u/nit

Dividing Syllables: Rules 6-10

When dividing syllables, divide between compound words.

sun/light   cob/web   cat/fish

When dividing syllables, digraphs (ck, ch, sh, th, wh) stay together.

ro/<u>ck</u>et

When dividing syllables, vowel teams (ai, ea, oa, oe, ee, ue, oo) stay together.

bal/l<u>oo</u>n

When dividing syllables, consonant blends (cl, thr, sp, str, sk, pr, lt, mp, dr, lf, ld) stay together.

sta<u>mp</u>/ing   <u>pr</u>e/sent   hun/<u>dr</u>ed

When dividing syllables, divide after a prefix (un, im, pre, in, re).

<u>un</u>/fair   <u>in</u>/spect   <u>pre</u>/pare

When dividing syllables, divide before the consonant + (le).

ap/<u>ple</u>   ea/<u>gle</u>   tur/<u>tle</u>

Unit 5
Resources

Punctuation

A <u>period</u> is for telling.

I like dogs.

An <u>exclamation</u> <u>mark</u> is for yelling.

Look at that dog jump!

A <u>question</u> <u>mark</u> is for asking.

How many times
can he jump?

Which do I use?

Will I tell, yell, or ask?

Apostrophes

Possessive nouns show that something is owned.
We use an apostrophe to show ownership.

Tonya's doll   Carlton's truck

Singular Possessives
When there is one owner, add an apostrophe + s. ('s)

Daddy's mug

when a singular possessive ends with s:

Proper noun: just add an (').
James'

Common noun add an ('s).
walrus's

Plural Possessives
When there is more than one owner, add an apostrophe after the s. (s')

 Turtles' shells

A **contraction** combines two words into one word.
We use an apostrophe in place of the missing letters.

I + **am** = I'm - Replace the (**a**) with an apostrophe (').

can + not = can't   does + not = doesn't   did + not = don't
are + not = aren't   have + not = haven't   is + not = isn't
do + not = don't   are + not = aren't
he + **is** = he's   she + **is** = she's   it + **is** = it's

Commas

Use a comma to separate the **city and state**.

We went to visit Orlando, Florida
and Atlanta, Georgia

Dates
Separate the day from the
year with a comma.

January 1, 2022

MAY 2025						
S	M	T	W	TH	F	S
				1	2	3
4	5	6	7	8	9	10
11	12	13	14	15	16	17
18	19	20	21	22	23	24
25	26	27	28	29	30	31

Use commas in **a series** to separate the items.
I bought apples, peaches, and lemons at the store.

Transition Words
Use a comma after a
transition word.

First,
Second,
Next,
Then,
Suddenly,

Opening and Closing
of a Letter
Use a comma after the
greeting and closing
of a letter.
Dear Mom,
I love you! Let's talk soon.
Sincerely,
Ray

Abbreviating Titles

An abbreviation is a shortened way to write a word.
Put a period at the end of most abbreviations.

Mister = **Mr.**   Misses = **Mrs.**   Senior = **Sr.**   Junior = **Jr.**

We can abbreviate positions of people.

Pastor = **Pr.**   Professor = **Prof.**   President = **Pres.**
Governor = **Gov.**   General = **Gen.**   Captain = **Capt.**

Abbreviating English Measurements

We can abbreviate liquid measurements.

teaspoon - **tsp.**   pint - **pt.**   quart - **qt.**   ounce - **oz.**
tablespoon - **tbsp.**   cup - **c.**   gallon - **gal.**   volume - **vol.**

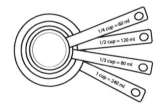

We can abbreviate solid measurements.

yard - **yd.**   foot - **ft.**   inch - **in.**   centimeter - **cm.**
mile - **mi.**   millimeter - **mm.**   meter - **m.**   pounds - **lb.**

0   1   2   3   4   5   6

Days of the week		Months of the Year	
Sunday	(Sun.)	January	(Jan.)
		February	(Feb.)
Monday	(Mon.)	March	(Mar.)
		April	(Apr.)
Tuesday	(Tues.)	May	(May)
		June	(Jun.)
Wednesday	(Wed.)	July	(Jul.)
Thursday	(Thurs.)	August	(Aug.)
		September	(Sept.)
Friday	(Fri.)	October	(Oct.)
		November	(Nov.)
Saturday	(Sat.)	December	(Dec.)

Nouns and Adjectives

A **noun** is a person, place, thing, or idea.

Person	Place	Thing	Idea

Matt	Egypt	Sailboat	Faith

Adjectives tell about nouns. Questions they answer:

What color?   What kind?   What size?   How many?

How does it look?   How does it taste?   How does it feel?

How does it behave?   What shape?   How does it smell?

My <u>hungry</u> dog looked at the <u>blue</u> bowl as he waited for food.

How does my dog feel? **hungry**   What color bowl? **blue**

Articles

Articles are words that come before a noun.
A, **an**, and **the** are articles.

a pony   an otter   the ostrich

Use (**an**) in front of a word that starts with a vowel sound.
Use (**a**) in front of a word that starts with a consonant sound.

a unicycle   **an** umbrella   **an** hour   **a** hat

Verbs and Adverbs

A **verb** is an action word.

run	jump	swim	hike

Adverbs describe verbs, adjectives and other adverbs.
Questions they answer:

How?   To what extent?   When?   Where?

verbs	**adjectives**	**adverbs**
He <u>selfishly</u> refused to share his candy.	He was really sweet to me <u>today</u>.	Tina slept <u>very</u> early.
How did he refuse?	When?	To what extent?
 selfishly	 today	very 

Simple Subjects and Predicates

Simple **Subject**	Simple **Predicate**
The simple subject is the noun (person, place, or thing) the sentence is about.	The simple predicate is the verb that tells about the subject.
Tom	cries

When we combine the simple subject and the simple predicate, we get a simple sentence.

Tom cries.

Complete Subjects and Predicates

Complete **Subject**	Complete **Predicate**
The complete subject is <u>all the words</u> that tell about the subject (noun).	The complete predicate is <u>all the words</u> that tell about the predicate (verb).
My dad's friend Tom	cried during the movie.

We combine the complete subject and the complete predicate to get a standard sentence.

 My dad's friend Tom cried during the movie.

Diagramming Sentences

The main part of the sentence, subject and predicate, go on the base line. We separate them with a vertical predicate line.

Wesley preaches.

predicate line

subject (noun) | predicate (verb)

Wesley | preaches

base line ➡

(Who or what the sentence is about.) (Tells the action to the subject)

Diagramming with Adjectives

We can diagram other parts of speech besides the subject and predicate. To diagram an adjective and article, write them on the diagonal lines underneath the base line on the subject side.

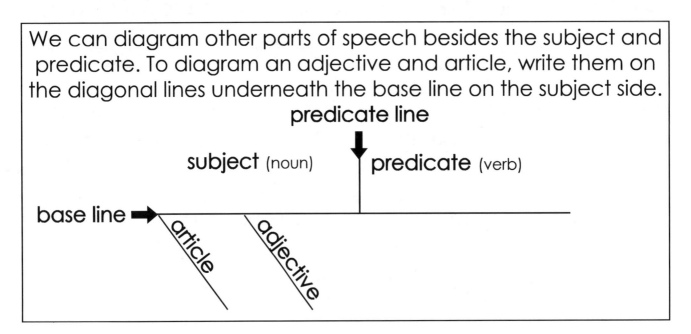

predicate line

subject (noun) | predicate (verb)

base line ➡

article adjective

Diagramming with Adverbs

We can diagram other parts of speech besides the subject, predicate, and adjectives. To diagram an adverb, write it on a diagonal line underneath the base line on the predicate side.

predicate line

subject (noun)   predicate (verb)

base line ➡

adverb

Diagramming with Article, Adjectives, and Adverbs

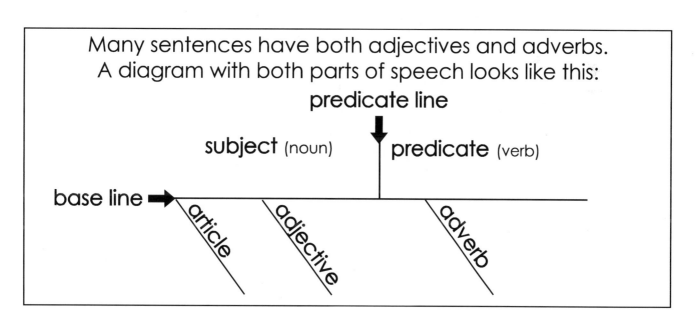

Many sentences have both adjectives and adverbs.
A diagram with both parts of speech looks like this:

predicate line

subject (noun)   predicate (verb)

base line ➡

article   adjective   adverb

Unit 6
Resources

Types of Writing

Opinion

An opinion is the way a person believes, thinks, or feels about a subject.

There are **four steps** to follow when writing an opinion piece:

1: Opinion	2: Reason	3: Examples	4: Opinion
Tell your reader how you feel about the subject.	Tell your reader why you feel that way about the subject.	Give your reader 2-3 examples for why you feel that way.	Restate your opinion for your reader.

Persuasive

Persuasive writing is written to convince the reader to agree with the author. It uses your opinion to influence others.

There are **four steps** to follow when writing a persuasive piece:

1: Belief	2: Point	3: Reasons	4: Belief
Tell the belief you want your reader to agree with.	Share at least 2 points with your reader for your belief.	Give 1-3 reasons why your reader should agree with your point.	Restate what you want your reader to agree with.

Informative

Informative writing is written to tell a reader about a specific subject. It does not try to convince a reader. It includes: facts, details, and explanations. Examples: reports, articles, how-to, invitations, recipes.

There are **four steps** to follow when writing an informative piece:

1: Topic	2: Topic Sentence	3: Facts	4: Conclusion
Choose a topic you want to talk about.	Write a topic sentence that tells what your topic.	Write at least 3 facts.	Write a sentence that sums it up.

Narrative

Narrative writing tells a story.

Personal Narrative:	Fictional Narrative:
...is a story that happened to you.	...is a make-believe story (not true).
...is based on true events.	...is written like a story.
...shows feelings and emotion.	...shows the feelings of the characters.

Types of Poems

Poetry is writing that creates feeling or emotions.

Color Poems	Sensory Poems
Poems that uses the senses to describe one color.	Poems that use all five senses to describe a feeling or thing.

Poetry elements you might see in these poems:

Line	Stanzas	Sensory Details
Words grouped together in one line in a poem.	Lines in a poem that are grouped together.	Using your senses to help your reader see

Acrostic Poems	Shape Poems
The first letter of each word spells out a word vertically.	Poems that are written in the shape they describe.

Cinquain Poems	Haiku Poems
A poem with five lines. Each line has a different number of syllables.	Poems that have three lines. The lines have a specific number of syllables each.

Poetry elements you might see in these poems:

Line	Line Break	Rhythm
Words grouped together in one line in a poem.	When a line ends and the reader pauses.	The pattern of the beat in a poem.

Rhyming Poems

Poems that have rhyming words, usually at the end of a line.

Poetry elements you might see in these poems:

Line	Repetition	Rhyme
Words grouped together in one line in a poem.	When a line is repeated.	Words in a poem that end with the same sound.

Types of Nonfiction Writing

Nonfiction writing is writing that is true. It is based on facts.

Letters
- writing that is sent from one person to another

Informational Text	Diaries/Journals	Essays/Articles
- articles - directions - textbooks	- writings about an author's day - includes thoughts and feelings	- writings about a specific topic - written to inform, persuade, or explain

Biography	Autobiography
- facts written about a person's life	- facts written about your own life.

Types of Fiction Writing

Fiction writing is writing that is make-believe.

Historical Fiction	Realistic Fiction	Fantasy
- A story that takes place in the past.	- A story that is not true, but could be true.	- A story that has impossible elements such as talking animals.

Folktales	Mystery	Adventure
* A story that is told from one generation to the next.	* A story that has clues and an event that is not understood.	*A story that risk, excitement, or danger

Writing Drama

Drama is a story (play) that is acted out by others.

Characters	**Narrator**	**Setting**
People in the play	Character in the play who tells the audience what is going on	When and where the play takes place

Script - written play which includes:

Dialogue	**Stage Directions**	**Act/Scene**
Words the characters speak. Use quotation marks. " "	Directions (where to go, how to move, when to speak) the actors follow	The play is divided into acts and scenes

Process of Writing
Prewriting

Prewriting is thinking!

Purpose	Topic	Brainstorm	Organize
What kind of writing will you be doing? Fiction or Nonfiction	What will you write about?	Write down as many ideas as you can about your topic.	Create a plan to put your writing in order.

1st Draft

A writer organizes ideas into sentences and paragraphs called a draft. The draft will change as the writer works to make it better.

As you write, check off what you've done:

characters ☑   setting ☑   problem ☑

solution ☑   complete sentences ☑

2nd Draft: Revise

Writers always reread their writing to make it better. They add words, change words and move things around to sound better.

Add details to your story. ☑   Change words to sound better. ☑

Remove words and sentences that don't make sense. ☑

Move words that would be better somewhere else. ☑

Use a ∧ to add words and —— to take away words. ☑

3rd Draft: Edit

Writers always go back and check for mistakes in spelling, capitalization, spacing, and punctuation.

Did you start each sentence with a capital letter?	yes	no
Did you end each sentence with punctuation (! . ?)?	yes	no
Did you circle words that you don't know how to spell?	yes	no
Did you write complete sentences?	yes	no
Did you put spaces between words and sentences?	yes	no

Publish

Are you ready to publish?

Did you rewrite your story using your best handwriting?	yes	no
Did you make all the changes from your revising?	yes	no
Did you make all the changes from your editing?	yes	no
Did you illustrate your story neatly?	yes	no
Are you ready to share your story with an audience?	yes	no

Narrative Writing: Prewriting

Fill out this graphic organizer to create a plan for writing.

Topic sentence

_____

_____

Five Senses

I saw:	I touched:	I tasted:	I heard:	I smelled:
_____	_____	_____	_____	_____
_____	_____	_____	_____	_____
_____	_____	_____	_____	_____
_____	_____	_____	_____	_____
_____	_____	_____	_____	_____

Inside Feelings and Thoughts

_____

_____

First, I _____	Next, I _____	Finally, I _____
_____	_____	_____
_____	_____	_____
_____	_____	_____
_____	_____	_____

Conclusion

_____

_____

Narrative Writing: 1st Draft

Use your prewriting to write a 1st draft.
Focus on writing complete sentences about your topic.

As you write, check off what you've done:

characters ☐   setting ☐   problem ☐

solution ☐   complete sentences ☐

2nd Draft: Revise
Use this revise checklist to make your 1st draft better.

Add details to your essay. ☐ Change words to sound better. ☐

Remove words and sentences that don't make sense. ☐

Move words that would be better somewhere else. ☐

Use a ∧ to add words and —— to take away words. ☐

3rd Draft: Edit
Use this editing checklist to make your 2nd draft better.

Did you start each sentence with a capital letter?   yes   no
Did you end each sentence with punctuation (! . ?)?   yes   no
Did you circle words that you don't know how to spell?   yes   no
Did you write complete sentences?   yes   no
Did you put spaces between words and sentences?   yes   no

Publishing a Narrative Writing
Writers publish their best work!

Are you ready to publish?

Did you rewrite your story using your best handwriting?   yes   no
Did you make all the changes from your revising?   yes   no
Did you make all the changes from your editing?   yes   no
Are you ready to share your story with an audience?   yes   no

Persuasive Writing: Prewriting

Brainstorm: Write down as many ideas as you can in 5 minutes.

What do you want to persuade people to do?

Fill out this graphic organizer.

What do you want to persuade people to do?

_____

_____

Point 1:

_____

_____

_____

Reason 1:	Reason 1:
_____	_____
_____	_____
Reason 2:	Reason 2:
_____	_____
_____	_____

Point 2:

_____

_____

_____

What do you want to persuade people to do?

_____

_____

Persuasive Writing: 1st Draft

Use your prewriting to write a 1st draft.

Focus on writing complete sentences about your topic.

As you write, check off what you've done:

persuasive topic sentence ☐   conclusion sentence ☐

point 1 ☐   reason 1 ☐   reason 2 ☐

point 2 ☐   reason 1 ☐   reason 2 ☐

2nd Draft: Revise

Use this revise checklist to make your 1st draft better.

Add details to your essay. ☐ Change words to sound better. ☐

Remove words and sentences that don't make sense. ☐

Move words that would be better somewhere else. ☐

Use a ∧ to add words and —— to take away words. ☐

3rd Draft: Edit

Use this editing checklist to make your 2nd draft better.

Did you start each sentence with a capital letter?   yes   no

Did you end each sentence with punctuation (! . ?)?   yes   no

Did you circle words that you don't know how to spell?   yes   no

Did you write complete sentences?   yes   no

Did you put spaces between words and sentences?   yes   no

Publishing a Persuasive Writing

Writers publish their best work!

Are you ready to publish?

Did you rewrite your story using your best handwriting?   yes   no

Did you make all the changes from your revising?   yes   no

Did you make all the changes from your editing?   yes   no

Are you ready to share your story with an audience?   yes   no

Informative Writing: Prewriting

Brainstorm: Write down as many ideas as you can in 5 minutes.

What subjects do you know a lot about?

Fill out this graphic organizer.

Topic: _____

_____

Topic Sentence: _____

_____

Fact 1:	Fact 2:	Fact 3:
____	____	____
____	____	____
____	____	____
____	____	____
____	____	____
____	____	____
____	____	____

Conclusion Sentence: _____

_____

_____

Informative Writing: 1st Draft

Use your prewriting to write a 1st draft.
Focus on writing complete sentences about your topic.

As you write, check off what you've done:

informative topic sentence ☐   conclusion sentence ☐

fact 1 ☐   fact 2 ☐   fact 3 ☐

2nd Draft: Revise

Use this revise checklist to make your 1st draft better.

Add details to your essay. ☐ Change words to sound better. ☐
Remove words and sentences that don't make sense. ☐
Move words that would be better somewhere else. ☐
Use a ∧ to add words and —— to take away words. ☐

3rd Draft: Edit

Use this editing checklist to make your 2nd draft better.

Did you start each sentence with a capital letter?	yes	no
Did you end each sentence with punctuation (! . ?)?	yes	no
Did you circle words that you don't know how to spell?	yes	no
Did you write complete sentences?	yes	no
Did you put spaces between words and sentences?	yes	no

Publishing an Informative Writing

Writers publish their best work!
Are you ready to publish?

Did you rewrite your story using your best handwriting?	yes	no
Did you make all the changes from your revising?	yes	no
Did you make all the changes from your editing?	yes	no
Are you ready to share your story with an audience?	yes	no

Sensory Poem

Write a sensory poem.
Start by writing the subject on the first line.

_____

_____ is _____

It tastes like _____

_____

It sounds like _____

_____

It smells like _____

_____

It looks like _____

_____

It feels like _____

_____

Color Poem

Write your own color poem.

_____

_____ is _____

_____ tastes like _____

_____ smells like _____

_____ sounds like _____

_____ feels like _____

_____ looks like _____

_____ makes me _____

_____ is _____

Cinquain Poem

Write your own cinquain poem.

Choose a noun and write everything you know about the noun.

_____
noun

_____   _____
adjective   adjective

_____   _____   _____
verb with -ing   verb with -ing   verb with -ing

_____ _____ _____ _____
four word phrase that describes the noun

_____
noun

Haiku Poem

Write a haiku poem.

_____

What is the poem about?

_____

Describe your word with **five syllables.**

_____

Describe your word with **seven syllables**

_____

Describe your word with **five syllables.**

Acrostic Poem

Write your own acrostic poem.

Draw a picture to go with it.

Shape Poem

First, write your shape poem on the lines. Then draw the outline of your shape and write the poem on the outline.

_____

_____

_____

_____

_____

_____